M000288286

the book of
NORDIC
self-care

the book of
NORDIC
self-care

Find peace and balance through seasonal rituals,
connecting with nature, mindfulness practices, and more

Elisabeth Carlsson

CICO BOOKS
LONDON NEW YORK

For my children Alvar, Clara, and Iris. Hope your Nordic spirit will always be with you.

Published in 2023 by CICO Books
An imprint of Ryland Peters & Small Ltd
20–21 Jockey's Fields   341 E 116th St
London WC1R 4BW   New York, NY
WC1R 4BW   10029

www.rylandpeters.com
10 9 8 7 6 5 4 3 2 1

Text © Elisabeth Carlsson 2023
Design, illustration, and photography
© CICO Books 2023
See page 143 for recipe, craft project,
and picture credits

The author's moral rights have been
asserted. All rights reserved. No part of this
publication may be reproduced, stored in a
retrieval system, or transmitted in any form
or by any means, electronic, mechanical,
photocopying, or otherwise, without the
prior permission of the publisher.

A CIP catalog record for this book is
available from the Library of Congress
and the British Library.

ISBN: 978-1-80065-266-8

Printed in China

Designer: Geoff Borin
Commissioning editor: Kristine Pidkameny
Editor: Jenny Dye
Art director: Sally Powell
Creative director: Leslie Harrington
Production manager: Gordana Simakovic
Publishing manager: Penny Craig

Notes

• The information in this book is not
intended to replace diagnosis of illness
or ailments, or healing or medicine.
Always consult your doctor or other
health professional in the case of illness
or for health or dietary advice.

• Both American (Imperial) and British
(Metric) are included in the recipes for
convenience. It is important to work with
one set of measurements only and not
alternate between the two within a recipe.

• All spoon measurements are level unless
otherwise specified. A teaspoon is 5ml,
a tablespoon is 15ml.

• All eggs are large (US) or medium (UK).

contents

introduction 6

chapter 1
natural health and beauty 10

chapter 2
nourishing food for all seasons 32

chapter 3
nature and forest 62

chapter 4
the home and seasonal living 84

chapter 5
a balanced life: nordic mindfulness 114

resources 136 · index 140

credits 143 · acknowledgments 144

introduction

The Nordic countries usually come in the top five happiest countries of the World Happiness Report. There are lots of reasons for this, but one of them is that, to a great extent, they feel safe for the individual. A lot of people don't distinguish between the Nordics and see them as a group of countries characterized by common ideas and values.

They include Denmark, Finland, Norway, Sweden, Åland, which is an autonomous region of Finland, and the Faroe Islands, a self-governing administrative overseas region of Denmark, and Greenland which is part of Denmark.

This is a book about self-care, inspired by the Nordic countries, their people, and their lifestyle, but also by what I brought with me from growing up in Sweden and, as so often is the way, only seeing the true value of that when other distractions lost their shine.

Nordic life is a lot about the small joys—not insignificant things but simple luxuries that don't cost a lot, such as free time, appreciating nature, and relaxation that doesn't involve trying to carve out time in a busy schedule, but is already built into everyday life. It's also about eating simple food that nourishes both your body and mind, creating a home with things that are functional yet beautiful, and having a lifestyle that moves away from consumerism toward sustainability and is supportive for both the natural world and the people that live in it. The Nordics' attitude to health is holistic, so they strive to find balance in most of its aspects—physical, mental, emotional, and spiritual well-being—and this shows up in all areas of their lifestyle. Nordic living includes choices that prioritize comfort and well-being, enjoying downtime and spending it with family and friends, taking care of the environment, and focusing on simplicity and practicality in the home but with attention to the details.

Knowing what your values are will affect where your attention goes and can help you to practice self-care without you even having to add it to your "to-do list." When we focus on the fundamentals of life and health, it's easier for us to stop and notice when things spiral out of control and we lose ourselves. When we grow our own food or at least appreciate the whole foods on our plates and where they came from, use natural materials when decorating our homes, and have comforting seasonal rituals around eating and cooking, that is a way of starting to slow down and show ourselves that self-care doesn't need a schedule.

But let's get back to basics—what does self-care even mean? The Oxford dictionary defines it as "The practice of taking an active role in protecting one's well-being and happiness, particularly during periods of stress." This means taking care of yourself to preserve your health, and it can't be measured externally or sold to you. Also, it means that everyone's self-care looks different. Start by asking yourself some questions and see how your body feels when you answer. For example, what first comes to mind when you ask, where do I feel rested? What activities help me feel calm and centered? What leaves me feeling frustrated and "deep fried?" What makes me feel stressed and what helps me regroup? What foods make my body feel good and supported? How does my home make me feel? How do I feel during moments of quiet and stillness? These are questions that will help you start to understand your parasympathetic nervous system (which

My mom and I out on a Sunday walk.

controls the body at rest), your body and environment, and ultimately, your own idea of well-being.

When we are stuck in a stressed mode, doing things that could improve our lives can lead to feelings of guilt because many of us associate self-care with self-indulgence and shame, as we just can't stick to new habits. By first truthfully examining those questions, the answers can usually be surprisingly simple. They usually land around wanting more peace, calm, and connection, and less distraction and stress. There is a fascination with the Nordic lifestyle, and it attracts many people who seek a different way of life based on a longing for more harmony and balance.

This book takes inspiration from the vast open spaces of the north, the dense forests, high mountains, and freshwater lakes and rivers; where you can find joy in eating berries straight off the bush that have been warmed by the sun, or foraging for mushrooms and cooking them outside; where you pare down your stuff—not only products you use for your skin and body but also things in your home—to reflect nature, where less is more and just being is enough.

Self-care is also about teaching yourself resilience, because it's easy to postpone "connecting with nature" outside on a gray, cold day in the winter until a sunny day comes around. Living seasonally and focusing on the possibilities rather than on the limitations of the weather is something that the Nordics do well, because there is beauty in the flow of a storm and the short days, just as there is in all seasons of life.

The Nordics can show us how to love our homes even more and create a place that makes us feel relaxed. Most people would probably admit that staying in is a bit of a luxury, so if you're not going out, make sure your home works for you, is inviting,

has lots of living plants, and helps you feel cozy and safe.

The Danish author Hans Christian Andersen once said, "The world is a series of miracles, but we're so used to them we call them ordinary things." Maybe self-care isn't about things that are grand, wild, and spectacular or cost money, but rather that daily walk in the park, learning to love nature in all its forms, knowing how to create a simple soup from seasonal ingredients without having to look at a recipe, decluttering a drawer, snuggling up with a soft wool blanket, and having your morning cup of tea outside while feeling the earth under your feet.

It's also a deep knowing that a connection to the landscape has an impact on your well-being. Finding a way of appreciating nature every day, whether you live in an urban environment or the countryside, is essential, and this book includes lots of tips on how to do this. Living in line with the natural world, whether through food, celebrations, planting seeds and watching them grow, bringing a flask of tea and something to eat outdoors, immersing yourself in natural waters, or having the scent from spring flowers wafting throughout your house, are all part of your self-care and your intention to live a more simple life.

chapter 1

natural health
and beauty

Fitness and staying healthy are generally big priorities for the people in the Nordics, and I can guarantee that if you chat to a Swede the conversation will eventually lead to them telling you about what they do for exercise or their latest health interest or outdoor pursuit. Being present, connecting with nature by practicing *friluftsliv* (see page 68), and staying active without pushing yourself in a gym is usually the Nordic approach to fitness. The same goes for beauty and skincare: the Nordics keep it simple, sustainable, and naturally sourced.

exercise and well-being

Self-care is all about looking after our needs, improving how we feel, and being resilient to events around us. It involves having simple daily routines which help to achieve some of these goals, and physical exercise is definitely up there as one of the core methods to increase your well-being. Research has shown that minimal movement is better than none, so just some gentle walking or even gardening can help. Often we get put off because we link exercise with the idea of losing weight, and lots of people have negative associations with this which is understandable. However,

exercise has numerous benefits that have nothing to do with stepping on a scale. For example, it improves cognitive function and makes your thinking sharper, as it stimulates the production of new brain cells. My son, who is now 15, is a prime example of this as when he started exercising and strength training in his last year of high school, his memory and grades improved and his teachers asked if he was the same boy. Movement is also protective against aging of the brain, as it increases the size of the hippocampus, which controls short-term memory.

By exercising you are also investing in yourself, which can help you feel powerful. Strength training and increasing muscle mass is key to reversing insulin resistance, which is critical in preventing diabetes, high blood pressure, and other metabolic diseases. The muscles are also the main reservoir of amino acids (the building blocks of protein). If we are unwell or being starved—think going on "diets"—the body relies on this ready supply in the muscles to make essential proteins. Having more muscle protects against osteoporosis as the bones grow stronger by bearing a heavy load, that is muscles. So you see, there are loads of benefits to exercise that won't have you checking your scales.

We all find it pretty hard to get out there and exercise regularly, but the Nordics don't seem to have this problem so much. It's thought their penchant for outdoor activities is related to the values of puritanical Lutheranism, which have historically been especially influential in Sweden and Norway. With the rise of consumerist individualism in other countries, the popularity of outdoor exercise has arguably suffered. Although, according to 2022 data from the Eurobarometer, which conducts surveys on behalf of the European Commission, the Nordic countries have the lowest value of non-exercising people, with just 8 per cent in Finland, 12 per cent in Sweden, and 20 per cent in Denmark, compared to 23 per cent in Germany and 45 per cent in France.

The high levels of people doing sporty activities outdoors in the Nordic countries probably also has something to do with the importance they place on being in nature. Outdoor exercise is widely believed to build character, and children from a young age in the Nordic countries are used to doing outdoor activities to boost fitness and resilience. The half-term school holidays in Sweden are even called *sportlov*, sporting holidays, which tells you all you need to know really. I remember orienteering fondly from my schooldays mainly because we were running around in the woods and could take cheeky breaks behind a pine tree. "For individuals who have not exercised for many years, the forest is a place with a low threshold," says Kati Vähäsarja, who has run Moved by Nature, a Finnish project promoting exercise in nature. Not only is it free or inexpensive, but it has so many brilliant advantages other than fitness—see page 68 for more on the Nordic concept of *friluftsliv* (free open-air life) and its benefits.

holistic skincare

For me, skincare and beauty have always been quite low key. I remember mixing together some herbs and water to make a face tonic as a teenager, because where I grew up there was a distinct lack of any kind of beauty store and I wanted to experiment beyond the soap my mom would buy.

I had to make do with the homemade stuff, using nature as my pharmacy and sourcing ingredients from plants, flowers, and the odd lump of clay too. A highlight in my teens was when my mom allowed me to order shower gel and lotions that used only natural ingredients from a French mail-order catalog—I was very excited when it finally arrived in the post.

Nordic skincare is very much inspired by nature and often contains locally sourced ingredients you cannot find elsewhere— think extracts from marine algae, nourishing tree sap, and antioxidant-rich berries. In order to endure conditions so far north, plants must adapt their defences—making for more potent ingredients. When used in skincare, these antioxidants make for powerful protection against free radicals that can cause various signs of skin aging.

Laura Heikkilä, who is the founder of Nörre Nordic, a Finnish company that focuses on skincare products says, "The Finnish people have a deep connection to nature. Finland… is the most forested country in Europe covering more than 75% of the land area… Finnish people are drawn to the natural beauty of the forest and are passionate about using natural ingredients in their skincare routine. Finnish forests are rich in unique wild plants, berries, and herbs that can't be found anywhere else on the planet. I think Finnish skincare is special because it takes advantage of these unique and potent ingredients that are abundant in the Nordic region. These ingredients have been used for centuries by our ancestors to nourish and protect the skin from the harsh weather conditions. Finnish skincare products often utilize ingredients straight

from the forest—like wild picked berries (e.g. lingonberry, cloudberry, bilberry, sea buckthorn, cranberry) and wild herbs (e.g. lady's mantle, nettle, meadowsweet, birch leaf)—to create products that are not only nourishing and gentle on the skin, but also highly effective in addressing specific skin concerns."

Reducing toxins in our environment is a key component of health. This is especially the case for women, as our hormones can easily be disrupted by too many chemicals and toxins, so seeking out natural body products can be one way to practice self-care. By doing this, we also put less of a burden on our environment.

Using natural ingredients and following a Nordic approach to holistic skincare—also considering lifestyle, diet, exercise, and stress levels—is the way forward, helping to achieve beauty that is radiant from the inside out. Choosing natural ingredients also applies to cleaning products for your house, because who needs a different bottle of cleaner for each type of dirt when one will do. My mom only ever used pine liquid soap for everything and I am pleased to say I can now find it in the UK.

A lot of new Nordic beauty brands focus on using sustainable ingredients and environmentally friendly packaging, reducing the impact on the planet. This comes from a deep respect for and connection to nature. Avoiding the depletion of natural resources is the key to sustainability and maintaining ecological balance. Laura Heikkilä says, "The rest of the world can certainly learn from the Scandi approach to skincare, as it emphasizes the importance of taking care of one's skin in a natural and sustainable way. By using locally sourced and minimally processed ingredients, Nordic skincare has a lower environmental impact while delivering effective results." She emphasizes that this holistic approach values simplicity, and focuses on the power of nature. This means that your skincare routine can be minimalistic and yet very effective.

The *lagom* (balanced) approach is at the core of Nordic beauty, and the balance of mind and body, and the internal and external, is inherent in a Nordic lifestyle. If you are healthy, your skin looks at its best. Look after yourself and increase your knowledge about what makes you feel good in terms of food, exercise, spending time outside, simple skincare, and enjoyment. Make a plan with a vision about what you believe a happy, balanced life should be. But be patient as nothing happens overnight, and embrace aging by focusing on staying strong and healthy.

creating a skincare routine

After many years of experimenting, using both very high-end and lower-end products, I find that less is definitely more. If you focus on restorative sleep, hydration and mineral-rich foods, lots of nature walks and natural light, your skincare routine can really be very simple. Use a gentle cleanser in the evening that doesn't disrupt the skin's barrier; I like the oil-cleansing method in the colder months. Then apply a simple plant-based oil such as jojoba or a serum, or nothing at all. In the morning, depending on the season and your skin type, wash only with water, followed by a tallow-based cream or a light lotion to moisturize.

STINGING-NETTLE TONIC

If you fancy making your own skincare, try this easy natural tonic recipe. Stinging nettles (*Urtica dioica*) are a flowering plant and have been used for their healing properties since ancient times. You can find stinging nettles in most parts of the world. Just avoid picking them where there is a lot of pollution and importantly, wear gloves to pick them. With an anti-inflammatory, anti-microbial, and astringent action, stinging nettles can help to reduce acne, fight skin infections, and reduce dark spots and redness. The tonic is also great for reducing inflammation, especially with burns. The cool thing with this beauty "concoction" is that you can also drink it as a tea. It's one of the most mineral-rich drinks you can have, which is a win-win for beauty inside and out.

1. Put 2 tablespoons of dried nettles in a pan of boiling water. If you are using fresh nettles, wash and dry them first, using gloves of course, then bunch a few stems together and leave them hanging up to dry for 1–3 weeks. You can also dry the nettles in the oven using the lowest setting for 3–4 hours, checking them regularly for dryness. Make sure you leave the oven door open a bit.

2. After boiling the nettles for 10 minutes, turn off the heat.

3. After it has completely cooled down, you can apply the tonic to your cleansed skin with the help of a cotton ball or reusable makeup pad. Store the tonic in a sealed container in the fridge for up to one week.

make-up

When it comes to make-up, keep things simple here too. The Nordic approach is generally minimal with fewer but better-quality products with high-quality formulas. It's rooted in good skincare and enhancing rather than trying to cover up, so less is more. It's about focusing on your natural features and being happy with what you have, rather than what you don't have.

sauna culture

Imagine sitting naked, in a heated room, with a bunch of strangers, getting sweaty. If someone then suggested whipping yourselves with a whisk made from tree branches, alarm bells would ring. For anyone who might not know of this traditional Finnish practice, and there might be a few out there, it could sound totally insane. Also, what does this have to do with self-care?

Finland was crowned the happiest place to live in 2020 and considering the weather, the lack of sunlight, and the fact that it's pretty cold for a lot of the year, it might make you wonder why. Of course, their brilliant health care, their school system, which is second to none, and their attitude to happiness are all relevant, but regular trips to the sauna could also have something to do with it. Finland is often seen as the birthplace of the sauna, but you can find similar traditions around the world.

The sauna, which means "bath house" in the Finnish language, is a product of prehistoric northern forest cultures, and in its most basic forms was probably originally used as both a dwelling and a bathing house. The first written references of saunas are found about 2000 years ago. Rocks would be placed in a pit in the ground and then heated by a fire. Water was then thrown on the rocks to create steam—the important *löyly*—which would give the sensation of increased heat. Later, wooden structures would be built around the rocks, creating what we now know to look like a sauna. Some people think that the word sauna comes from the Finnish word *savuna*, which means "in smoke," and *savusauna* is the type of sauna that doesn't have a chimney, which is the original kind of sauna structure. The sauna was also a big component in all major events of the year, and it was during these special times that the Finns believed spirits bathed in the sauna. Over the ages the sauna has served many functions for the Finnish people, including curing meat, healing the sick, and even for childbirth. Tiina Knauttiila, a program manager from Finland now living in Spain, says "it was

once called the 'poor man's pharmacy'…
the tarring of the wood inside the sauna
prompting the proverb 'if liquor, tar and
sauna won't help, an illness is fatal'."

Visiting a sauna is a tradition that is
deeply ingrained in the Finnish culture.
With 3.2 million saunas in a country of
5.5 million people, it is often said that the
entire Finnish population would be able
to go to a sauna at the same time at any
given moment. Many Finnish people have
a sauna at home or at their holiday house,
and generally think that a cottage without
a sauna is not a holiday getaway at all. Even
the Finnish Parliament has one. In Finland
as well as in Sweden, public swimming
pools and spas will always have a sauna.
In the past, public saunas were shut down

and almost disappeared in the 1950s but recently, sauna culture has grown and many new ones are being built.

Sauna culture involves much more than simply sitting in a warm space enjoying the *löyly* (steam) and the *vihtu* (see page 25). In a sauna, people cleanse both their bodies and minds and embrace a sense of inner peace. Traditionally, the sauna has been considered a sacred space—a "church of nature."

Twenty minutes spent in a sauna can be one of the best things you can do for your self-care, helping you to de-stress and relax. When you step into the sauna, the air envelops you like a warm hug and after a while you will notice that the space is still and peaceful. Most people sitting in a sauna don't speak—it's as if you all are just coming together silently, contemplating life, and there is no need for small talk. The effects of the heat and the silence, with only your thoughts to occupy you, can be a bit overwhelming at first, especially as we are so used to always being on the go. The longer you stay, the more you will feel that you can press pause on your hectic schedule. This sensation of an internal pause is something you will bring with you for a while after you leave.

Heat-based therapies have been used across the globe for thousands of years. There are records of Mayans, Romans, ancient Greeks, and Aboriginal elders using them. Here are six benefits that show how saunas can be a great way of practicing self-care—if you have the chance, give it a go.

1. Saunas can ease pain and aid in recovery from injury. The increased blood flow you get from the heat in the sauna helps to speed up the body's natural healing processes. When the heat relaxes your muscles, it improves circulation, and the body releases endorphins, which act like a mild tranquilizer.

2. It can help with that dreaded yearly flu. The heat helps the body to create white blood cells, which are the cornerstones of our immune system. When you are less stressed, you are more likely to ward off illnesses as your body has more energy to fight them. The *löyly* can help to reduce nasal and sinus congestion. It's also common to add some eucalyptus oil to a sauna, for some extra spa-like self-care. It should be said that if you have a fever, you shouldn't use a sauna.

3. Studies show that there is a large reduction in all-cause mortality by those who use regular saunas of 174°F (79°C). Regular sauna use is protective against the risk of cardiovascular disease and heart attacks in men. The heat increases the heart rate to 100 beats per minute during regular sauna bathing sessions, and to 150 beats per minute during more intense warm sauna bathing. This corresponds to low and moderate-intensity physical exercise. Similarly, evidence also show that blood pressure may be lower among those who live in warm conditions.

4. Saunas can improve brain health. The Alzheimer's Association has sweating on its list as a way to improve brain health, and a 20-year study at University of Eastern Finland revealed that regular sauna use of 4 to 7 times per week at 176°F (80°C) for 19 minutes per session lowered the risk for Alzheimer's and dementia.

5. Saunas can also help with sleep. This happens because of endorphins that are released, but is also to do with a falling body temperature following the sauna session. Ideally you would have a sauna 1–2 hours before going to sleep as the combination of endorphins and a falling body temperature makes you sleep easier and deeper.

6. They help to improve skin health. For anyone who has been to a hammam (Turkish bath), during a scrub by one of the staff, you might have experienced the amount of dirt that rolls of your skin, which is kind of unpleasant at first but gives you beautiful skin. The sauna steam makes you sweat out bacteria and dead skin cells trapped in the epidermal layer of your skin, and cleans your pores as well. This improves your capillary circulation and makes your skin healthier.

as being used to gently lash your skin, it acts like a fan to increase air circulation by mixing the hot and cold layer in a sauna to increase the heat. The branches also act like a natural form of aromatherapy. You could use birch, eucalyptus, or oak. Different trees have different purposes; oak, for example, is suited to oily skin and is a very strong anti-inflammatory agent. Eucalyptus is anti-inflammatory, anti-bacterial, and supports your respiratory system. Birch is also anti-inflammatory, acts like a soap, and is used to wash dirt and grease off the skin.

vihtu

Lastly, what about the branches of birch, the *vihtu*, otherwise known as the sauna whisk. This needs to be soaked in water before use and serves various functions. As well

fjord focus

Water and the Nordic people are deeply interconnected. It's well known that there are a lot of lakes across Scandinavia, but did you know that Finland is known as the land of a thousand lakes? This is not surprising as there are actually 188,000 lakes in Finland, and Helsinki has around 330 islands in its archipelago. Stockholm is built on 14 islands, which are all interconnected by 57 bridges. Copenhagen started out as a fishing village and its many canals are evidence of that, and Denmark has over 5400 miles (8700km) of coastline, meaning you are never far from water. Oslo is at the end of a fjord, and Reykjavik means "Smoky Bay" in Old Norse, a name said to be inspired by the steam rising from hot springs.

With the proximity to water, kayaking, sailing, kite surfing, swimming, and river rafting are all very common pursuits in the Nordic countries. In fact, one of my favorite holiday memories from growing up in Sweden was doing a canoe hike with friends and sleeping outdoors. On one of the warm

sunny afternoons, we tied all of our canoes together and just lay down in them, gently drifting with the lapping of the water. If you are looking for something a bit more challenging, the fjords of Western Norway offer some of the most breathtaking kayaking routes, where you can paddle past waterfalls and right into the heart of Trondheim.

If you fancy a swim in the Nordic countries, you are clearly never far from a lake, the sea, or, if you are in Iceland, a hot spring or swimming pool. Thanks to Iceland's geothermal heat, swimming is a national institution and nearly every

town has a heated swimming pool or *sundlaug*, often outdoors. Most pools also offer a *heitir pottar*—a small heated pool for soaking—with a water temperature of about 104°F (40°C) and also saunas and hot tubs. This connection to water is not exclusive to the Nordics, because who doesn't feel relaxed near a lake or by the sea, but the difference is that the Nordics appreciate the water in all seasons and at all opportunities. When we are by water, our brains enter into a relaxed "mode," which in turn has an effect on our creativity as our thoughts have a chance to flow without any

external interruption. The brain probably also recognizes the ancient connection we all have with water and the sea, and that in itself makes us relax.

"Blue Mind" science explores the idea that water is the primary source of well-being, and it was coined by the marine biologist Wallace J. Nichols in his book *Blue Mind*. It is the study of aquatic environments' health benefits. It is also linked to blue-colored objects which symbolize water and have been shown to have a similar effect on the brain. Wallace says in his book *Blue Mind*, "We are drawn to water, because we come from, and are still largely made of water. In fact, the human body is about 60 percent water, and the brain is 75 percent water." Interestingly, the planet is also made up of 75 percent water. "When you see water, when you hear water, it triggers a response in your brain that you're in the right place," Wallace says.

Simple things such as taking a shower or a bath have a positive influence on our senses, including our mind. Scientist have known for years that the atmosphere at a beach or near to moving water contain high levels of negatively charged ions. According to Pierce J. Howard, PhD, author of *The Owner's Manual for the Brain*, these negative ions increase the flow of oxygen to the brain, which can decrease drowsiness and make you more alert and energetic. Using techniques such as MRI scans, researchers have shown that proximity to

water increases our levels of "feel-good" hormones such as dopamine and oxytocin, and levels of the stress hormone cortisol drop, helping us to relax even more. The scientific evidence now validates Nichols' concept of the blue mind, as well as what we instinctively feel when we are close to the water.

cold dipping

Cold-water swimming or ice bathing has become a massive trend in the last few years—you literally cannot escape all the posts about people jumping into ice baths in freezing temperatures.

The proponents of cold-water swimming list many reasons why it is beneficial, and one of them is that it activates our brown adipose tissue. Our bodies have both white and brown fat. One of the things that affects how many calories we burn every day and our risk of obesity, regardless of how we exercise and what we eat, is how activated our brown fat cells are. Brown fat also increases our metabolic rate and has a direct effect on our body temperature. Babies and young children have much more brown fat than adults do, because they can't yet shiver in response to being cold to regulate their body temperature, so they must rely on brown fat to turn up their body heat. However, adults do hold on to some brown fat throughout their whole lives.

Fredrik Nystrom, a professor and doctor at Linköping University in Sweden, carried out a study about the effects of cold therapy on the body and the results show that the brown fat is very much a main player here. This is not an experiment I would like to have done myself, but I am glad that some people did in the name of science. The participants were exposed to cold temperatures for one hour per day for six weeks, and their brown fat was measured before and after. The brown fat around their collarbones increased and the participants reported a much better ability to keep warm during the winter. The study also showed that participants who kept warm during the study did not increase their brown fat; instead, their metabolic rate lowered.

When we first get over the fight or flight response and get our breathing sorted, going from a sharp in breath to a slow and calm in-and-out, that is when we can start to reap the positive effects of cold-water swimming. At that point, the stress hormone cortisol is released from your adrenal glands while endorphins are increased in your brain. Endorphins provide powerful pain relief and can give you a feeling of euphoria. So if you can learn to adapt to the cold water, which reduces our general stress response, you can then potentially lessen your risk for and reduce signs of depression.

However, as with most things it's key to find balance—that sweet spot that increases well-being and doesn't become another stressful thing in the diary or for your body. The Swedish *lagom* (balanced) attitude is a good approach here. Yes, it is great that cold-water swimming can make you smile, increase your resilience, and prevent you from sinking into a low mood. We all want a simple solution to our problems, and for some, cold-water swimming has been just the ticket. However, what the body wants more than anything is homeostasis (stability), and constantly putting your body in intense stressful experiences can have a detrimental effect on your physiology and even increase aging due to the increased stress hormones, such as adrenaline.

Just because something becomes very popular doesn't mean it works for everyone. What is important to understand is bio-individuality—the idea that we are all born with varied tolerances to life's stressors. If we see someone who can seemingly handle extreme stressors and do well, it doesn't mean they become healthier. So when it comes to cold-water swimming, as with anything that is suddenly popular, think about whether you are doing it because you enjoy it. If you are making yourself do it just because you think it's good for you, that is the opposite of self-care.

However, I think the key benefit of cold-water swimming is that it is a simple activity that you do with other people in a natural environment. A study by the University of York that came out in 2021 reinforces the idea that a group activity that is performed regularly for at least 2–3 months has the most positive effect. "The main theory of the study was that nature-based activities… help us connect to nature in a meaningful way rather than passively observe nature," explains the lead author Peter Coventry. A comment from a friend of mine who started cold dipping during the pandemic illustrates this fact perfectly. She says, "It's just such a lovely way to connect with people as it doesn't take a lot of organization and you can count on there usually being people by the beach in all seasons." For more on wild swimming and tips on how to get started, turn to page 75.

chapter 2

nourishing food for all seasons

The Nordic diet is all about eating whole, unprocessed foods, with an emphasis on mindfulness and an absence of stress around mealtimes. It is not universally followed but on the whole, it forms the basis of how most people eat in the Nordic countries.

It consists of fresh whole foods, locally sourced and seasonal produce, and ingredients that are high in nutrients. It also contains lots of fruit, berries, seasonal vegetables, wholegrains—the Nordics love their bread—and of course plenty of fish and dairy. The Nordic diet is also very much based around salted, cured, pickled, and fermented foods, due to the weather and the long cold season when it's not possible to grow or pick fresh foods.

Self-care is often about balance and this is never more true than when it comes to food. Diet culture is everywhere today, and it's not uncommon to have lots of rules about what we should and shouldn't eat, putting food into categories of "good" or "bad." However, quite often going on a strict diet with the aim of only losing weight can deprive you of important food groups. There is no balance or self-care in following a strict regime. Food should not only feed our hunger but on a deeper level also bring us joy and nourishment in equal measure. Self-care is often talked about in terms of activities that we might only do sometimes,

such as a massage, a fancy retreat, or a bath, but what about those things we need to do daily, such as eating—this is where the biggest gains can be had.

We might think that self-care around food is about making the most nutritious choices, but we all know it's so much more than that. Food and eating are also very much connected to our families and our childhoods. This link we have with our past is what we bring into our own lives and into the future when raising our families. Linn Thorstenson, a Swedish nutritionist now living in Ireland who specializes in disordered eating says, "Self-care is first and foremost to recognize that you are hungry and the need to actually eat. When we start listening to our bodies we can then start to understand more about what our needs really mean, what the body telling us… when we practice self-care with food, we can start to meet our needs in a completely different way and how that fits into the bigger picture of family, home, comfort, joy and excitement."

cooking through the seasons

It's clear that in recent years the Nordic region has embraced world cuisine and different cooking techniques. The Nordic diet has partly moved away from the traditional foods of my childhood, and the emphasis now is very much on health.

The food of my childhood was traditional Swedish *husmanskost* (home-cooked food), with not a single garlic clove in sight. When I was growing up, the farm freezer, cellar, and larder were stacked with ingredients sourced from the land and forest. We ate things such as oven pancakes with crispy bacon, cooked hen and rice, meat loaf (yes, not meatballs because who's got time for that when you have five children), moose stew, *slottstek* potroast, *Kardemumma bullar* (cardamon buns—not cinnamon because my dad didn't like the taste). There were also potatoes daily and lots of bread and coffee. The flavors were simple, only seasoned using salt, black and white pepper, all spice, and maybe some snippets of dill and chives. Although an attempt into more exotic flavors was the Spice Island spice mix on our pork chops in the 1970s and '80s.

At the heart of it though, the Nordic diet is very much about seasonal and local foods. Respect for sustainability, raw ingredients, and for what can be foraged run deep, because of course until recently not everything was available in the Nordic region. The Nordics like to cook and see this skill as essential basic knowledge. This is like a thread that runs through the Nordics and explains a lot of their choices when it comes to cooking and eating. Food to me is heavily connected to seasons, and most Nordic children have an innate understanding of what foods are in season when. This knowledge partly comes from home economics education that is part of most Nordic schools' curriculums, but also just from being involved in foraging and preparing food from a young age.

seasonal celebrations

Just as with seasonal decorations in the house, the Nordics also excel at celebrations with particular foods, and they even have songs for each holiday or season. Honouring special occasions is one way of cultivating a sense of community, because you know that most people in your region tend to celebrate these days in the diary. These celebrations are a direct product of cultural background, history, and religious beliefs, and commemorating special occasions has been going on from the dawn of humanity. Seasonal celebrations also help to place a mental bookmark at various points in the year when you can gather your loved ones, make special foods and drinks (such as the *glögg* recipe opposite), and perhaps decorate your home. Knowing that these occasions come again every year creates a sense of safety and security; they are something to look forward to and give you a break from the mundane routine.

With global travel and most people not living in their birthplace or even birth country, a lot of people might not mark the seasonal traditions that they grew up with. However, rituals that come from your heritage might be something that you can pass on to your children. In our Anglo-Swedish home, we have a bit of a mix of traditions that are special just to our household. We make a point of eating seasonal dishes, usually involving herring, around Christmas, Easter, and Midsummer for example, because that is how I was brought up. My children are used to the flavors of my upbringing such as dill, sweet and sour pickles, and fish. They are also used to foraging for nettles in the Spring, eating the soup I make, and picking berries to make jam and cordials.

However, when they have families of their own some of those traditions will stick and they might introduce new ones themselves. But the concept of marking the seasons with food is one that I hope they will take with them, as it creates a kind of mindfulness around preparing and eating foods for special occasions. Those traditions also help to strengthen family connections, and to connect past and future generations. Humans have a need to hand down traditions through the ages. This helps both children and adults feel a sense of belonging, which is why embracing seasonal recipes can be an act of self-care.

GLÖGG

Glögg is the Scandinavian version of mulled wine, and is enjoyed throughout the Nordic countries during the winter season and especially on Sundays in Advent (see page 94).

1 orange

two 3-cup (750ml) bottles dry red wine (the quality doesn't matter)

¾ cup (200ml) aquavit or vodka

12 cardamom pods, crushed

8 cloves

1¼in (3cm) piece of fresh ginger, sliced

1 cinnamon stick

1½ cups (250g) sugar

1⅓ cups (200g) raisins

1¼ cups (200g) blanced almonds

Serves 20

Using a vegetable peeler, remove the zest form the orange in a single curl (do not include any of the bitter white pith). Put all the ingredients, except the almonds, in a large stainless-steel or enamel saucepan.

Just before serving, heat to just below boiling point. (Do not let the liquid boil or the alcohol will be burned off.) Remove from the heat and stir in the almonds.

Serve in glass punch cups or tea glasses, with small spoons so that the softened almonds and raisins can be scooped out and eaten.

the Nordic diet

Planning, shopping, and cooking can be overwhelming, but sticking to whole food ingredients, following what's in season, and knowing a handful of simple recipes that you can repeat weekly is key to supporting your self-care around food.

By adding a few candles, extra plates of raw vegetables, and crackerbread and butter, each meal becomes more well-rounded on every level. On the following pages you'll find inspiration from across the Nordic region. There are some similarities between the Nordic countries, but they all have their unique traditions and foods.

Faroe Islands

The cuisine here is all about lamb, root vegetables such as carrots and kohlrabi, potatoes, and rhubarb—all things that can grow easily in the Faorese harsh climate. On the menu you can often find *skærpikjøt* (dried lamb) and dried *ræst* cod; both of these are foods that most families would eat weekly. People in the Faroe Islands are very hospitable and will often host tourists in their houses for dinner. They even have a word for this tradition—*Heimablídni*—where

guests pay to experience traditional meals in local people's homes. The word itself means "home hospitality" and refers to authentic dining experiences—local food that's combined with interesting stories about the village where *heimablídni* is held.

Iceland

This country is surrounded by water so it's no surprise that most traditional Icelandic food revolves around fish, as well as dairy, bread, potatoes, and lamb. Their *kjötsúpa* (lamb soup) is a bit of a national dish. They also favor dried meat—*hangikjot* and dried fish—*hardfiskur*. Most families have a version of fish stew called *plokkfiskur* which is either cod or haddock with boiled potatoes. *Skyr* is an Icelandic yogurt and has become popular around the world. It's even mentioned in the Icelandic sagas (prose narratives based on historical events that took place among the Norse and Celtic inhabitants in the ninth, tenth and eleventh centuries), and no doubt helped with growing strong Vikings. Ice cream is a bit of a thing too in Iceland, and when my son Alvar went there for a school trip, one of the nicest ice creams he's had is forever etched in his memory.

KJÖTSÚPA (lamb soup)

This rustic, simple soup uses lamb or mutton and root vegetables. It has legendary healing powers and is perfect for a dark winter's night, especially if you've been out for a hike. This soup is so healthy, providing calcium, collagen, and glycine. Traditional cultures have always included bones, tendons, and cartilage in their soups and this sort of food builds strong people.

The meat is braised and creates its own stock. It has little seasoning other than salt, pepper, and Icelandic herbs including dried parsnips, carrot, and leek, which are sold as "soup herbs" at Icelandic grocery stores. You can add thyme and oregano instead. Most families will have their own version of this dish but here is a basic one for you to try.

18oz (500g) rutabaga/swede, peeled

18oz (500g/4 medium-sized) potatoes, peeled

9oz (250g/4 medium-sized) carrots, peeled

piece of leek/a few parsnips, peeled (optional)

35oz (1kg) lamb on the bone, such as shoulder. Trim off the fat and cut it into a few pieces.

1 tablespoon Icelandic salt or sea salt, plus extra for seasoning at the end (Icelandic salt is the least contaminated on earth, so it's worth seeking out)

½ tsp each oregano and thyme, or a few sprigs of each

half an onion, finely chopped

3½oz (100g) cabbage, sliced, or kale

⅓ cup (80g) rice or ⅓ cup (30g) rolled oats, if you would like a heartier soup

freshly ground black pepper

Serves 4–6

Cut the rutabaga or swede, potatoes, carrots, and leek or parsnips (if using) into similar size chunks. Make sure they aren't too small.

In a large pot, brown the lamb all over on a medium–high heat. Pour in 1¾ pints (1.5l) water, or enough to just cover the meat, and bring to the boil. Use a spoon to skim the scum off the top and add the tablespoon of salt and the rice or oats, if using.

Add the herbs and onion, simmer for another 50 minutes, then add the swede, potatoes, carrots, and leek or parsnips (if using), and simmer for another 20 minutes until they are soft. Remove the meat and the bones from the soup, roughly chop the meat, and return to the pot. Season to taste with salt and pepper. Serve with unlimited bread and butter.

Norway

Norwegians love their fish and eat it multiple times a week. They also use potatoes a lot, including in baking. During the Napoloeonic wars, flour was rationed and potatoes were used in baking as a substitute. Their chubby flatbread, *lomper*, also known as *stomp* or *potetkaker* and the thinner and larger *Lefse* are both made from a mixture of flour and cooked potatoes. You use them as a wrap and fill them with delicious ingredients such as a *pølser* (sausage) maybe alongside a beer. The Norwegians love the outdoors so much they even have a name for the beer they drink outside—"*utepils.*"

LOMPER (flatbread)

14oz (400g) floury potatoes (such as King Edward), peeled and cut into small chunks

1 teaspoon sea salt

2 tablespoons unsalted butter

9oz (250g) barley flour

2 baking trays, lined with non-stick baking parchment

Makes about 20 flatbreads

Boil the potatoes for 10–15 minutes, or until tender. Drain, leave to cool and reserve 200ml of the cooking liquid.

Preheat the oven to 475°F (250°C) Gas 9.

Denmark

You can't go to Denmark without trying the *smørrebrød*, an open sandwich. There are many versions of it, and its toppings include herring, smoked salmon, meat, liver paté, eggs, and pickled beets. The bread varies from white to dark rye. My particular favorite is the *kartoffelmad*, sliced cold potato, and potato connoisseurs will argue it's best in June or July when the *frilandskartofler*, free range potatoes, are in season. I particularly love them on some crackerbread with a few snipped chives.

Add the salt and butter to the potatoes with most of the reserved cooking liquid. Mix to make a smooth, soft mixture. Set aside to cool down a little.

Add the flour to the cooled potato mixture—you should have a firm but pliable dough. Add a little more of the reserved cooking liquid if the dough is too stiff.

Pull off pieces of dough about the size of plums, and roll into balls between your hands. Place on a prepared baking tray and flatten with your hands or a floured rolling pin to make thin discs. Prick all over with a fork. You will need to bake the flatbreads in batches because they will not all fit on the baking trays.

Bake in the preheated oven for 15 minutes, or until golden brown with some darker patches.

Sweden

The cuisine here is about more than meatballs, even though most households, especially those with kids, have them at least once a week alongside a helping of macaroni pasta and a good squirt of ketchup. This also makes brilliant picnic food by the way. The Swedes eat *husmanskost*, which refers to traditional home-cooked food, although this is now very much mixed with global tastes and dishes. Eating tacos is a given every Friday when everyone does *fredags mys*—a cozy Friday evening in. Potatoes feature heavily in the Swedish diet, especially new potatoes in July and August, fish and herring of course, lots of fermented dairy, and bread, especially the cracker kind. We also love our *fika*, the natural coffee break that everyone stops for throughout the day, alongside a small snack or sandwiches. Sandwiches are a staple, especially on rye bread with various cold cuts or *pålägg*, and fresh or pickled cucumber on top. Anyone who has read *The Girl with the Dragon Tattoo* knows that the detective especially favors cheese and orange marmalade sandwiches and this is also my favorite. The Swedes also love their baked sweet breads, cinnamon rolls being the most well-known. They even have a special day for it—*Kanelbullens dag* on October 4th.

GRÖTBULLAR (no-waste porridge rolls)

Swedes love their porridge for breakfast, bread rolls for sandwiches, and are big on no waste. This recipe combines the three because who doesn't have porridge left over in the morning. I often throw this simple dough together in the morning and sometimes leave it to prove until the afternoon to bake. It's very forgiving.

For the porridge
(if you don't have leftovers)

7oz (200g) porridge oats

12fl oz (350ml) water

2oz (50g) butter

For the bread

1 teaspoon dried yeast or ¾oz (25g) fresh yeast

1¾lb (800g) plain flour or 18oz (500g) strong white flour

8¾fl oz (250ml) milk

1½ teaspoons salt

2 tablespoons golden syrup (I sometimes add a bit more because I like the slightly sweet/savoury taste)

Makes 12–14

Mix the porridge ingredients in a saucepan, bring to the boil, then simmer gently until you get a smooth porridge. If it's too thick or stodgy, add some more water. If you are using leftover porridge, add some water and

simmer. You will need about 7oz/
7fl oz (200ml/200g) of porridge. Melt the
butter straight in the pan with the leftover
porridge. Leave the porridge to cool.

If you are using fresh yeast, dissolve this in
the milk first in a large mixing bowl. Then
mix in the rest of the bread ingredients
and the cooled porridge. If you are using
dried yeast, add straight to the flour in a
large mixing bowl, then mix in the rest
of the bread ingredients and the cooled
porridge. The dough will be a little bit wet
and it doesn't need much kneading. If it
is too dry, add a drop of water or milk and
just make sure the dough comes together.
Cover the dough with a towel (sometimes I
put it in a plastic bag). Leave to prove for an
hour at room temperature, until it's roughly
doubled in size. Push the dough with your
finger. If it doesn't spring back, it's ready.

Tip the dough out of the bowl and divide it
into two pieces. The dough might be sticky,
but try not to use too much flour to dust
it. Roll each piece until it is about 12–16in
(30–40cm) long. Use a dough cutter to
cut each piece into 8–10 pieces. You can
shape them into round shapes, but it's not
necessary. Pop the pieces on a baking tray
lined with baking parchment, leave to prove
for about 30 minutes at room temperature,
then bake for 12–15 minutes in an oven
at 450°F (230°C) Gas 8. Cool on a griddle
under a cloth. The rolls freeze well and can
be defrosted as and when you want them.

KLADDKAKA

I highly recommend adding this Swedish sticky chocolate cake to your repertoire, as it is so easy to make and it always turns out delicious.

2 eggs

1 cup (200g) superfine (caster) sugar

1 cup (150g) all-purpose (plain) flour

3 tablespoons good-quality cocoa powder, plus extra for dusting

1 tablespoon vanilla sugar or extract

pinch of salt

1 stick (100g) unsalted butter, melted and cooled slightly

whipped cream, to serve

8-in (20-cm) deep round cake pan, greased and lined with baking parchment

Preheat the oven to 350°F (180°C) Gas 4.

Whisk the eggs and sugar together until the mixture is light, fluffy, and pale.

Sift all the dry ingredients into the egg and sugar mixture. Fold in until everything is incorporated, then fold in the melted butter. Pour into the prepared cake pan.

Bake in the preheated oven for around 10–15 minutes. The exact time can vary, so keep an eye on the cake. A perfect kladdkaka is very, very soft in the middle, but not runny once it has cooled –but almost runny. The cake will not rise, but it will puff up slightly during baking.

If you press down gently on the cake, the crust should need a bit of pressure to crack. When this happens, the cake is done. Leave to cool in the pan. Serve with whipped cream, dusted with cocoa powder.

Finland

Not too dissimilar to their neighbors, the Finns eat seasonally and many of their ingredients are sourced from the thousands of forests and lakes that Finland is so well-known for. This means that many of the popular dishes are seasonal—new potatoes (*uudet perunat*) will be on the early summer table, berries such as lingon and blueberries are eaten in early fall, then mushrooms in late fall, and during the long winter, lots of root vegetables such as swede, carrot, and of course cabbage. Meat and fish feature too, including reindeer and salmon. Porridge is the backbone of a Finnish breakfast or you could also try *Vispipuuro*, which is a version where you whisk lingonberries and semolina together. Rice porridge is also quite common and leftovers of this can be used in Finland's most popular snack, Karelian pie. Finns also love pancakes or *pannukakku*, and they are on the menu every Thursday following their pea soup. They also cook their pancakes in the oven, which creates a thicker version, and my Finnish neighbour Marika also makes green ones in a pan, which is a very clever way to get your kids to eat spinach.

kaffe paus

Coffee deserves its own section, as the Nordics drink more of that hot black stuff than most other countries.

The Finns are at the top of the list with their vast consumption of *kahvia*. They drink it all day long, alongside some kind of snack such as the Finnish version of a cinnamon roll, *pulla* bread. Norwegians come next, and they might even have a cheeky *karsk*, which is a cocktail of weak coffee, sugar, and some moonshine, i.e. some vodka. They also love their traditional boiling coffee or *kokekaffe*, ideally made in a kettle (*på bål*) over a fire when they are out in nature.

The people in Iceland love their coffee so much that it plays a big role in Iceland's folklore. For example, they have the saying *þrælapar*, which means that if you serve a guest a cup of coffee with a saucer that does not match, then the guest will have to remarry or have an affair. The Danes are fourth on the list with their *hyggeligt* coffee, which they drink in cozy cafes, and the Swedes, sixth on the list with their *fika*, which involves taking lots of time out to enjoy *kaffe*, mostly filter coffee, and some kind of bready snack.

What we can learn from the Nordics' way of drinking coffee is to have the coffee and snack combo—so never drink it on an empty stomach to avoid blood-sugar crashes. Also try to have the best coffee you can to reap more benefits. Revving the nervous system with too much caffeine is not self-care in my book, but stopping for a break a few times a day while having a snack is.

nature's bounty— foraging

A strong memory from my childhood is hours of boredom out in the woods, fighting off midges, and looking for berries. I say "boredom" because quite often what you have on your doorstep is not that interesting, especially in your teenage years.

However, now I am very grateful for those experiences as they taught me to appreciate nature and seasonal foods before living in cities for the best part of my adulthood. A big part of those forest excursions was foraging and looking for edibles in the forest, spotting "nature's gold" among the dark parts of the woods, including mushrooms and especially chantarelles. We would pick berries using a brilliant *bärplockare*, a nifty berry-picker invention that makes berry picking, especially for *lingon* (see image on page 52) and *blåbär*, so much easier. Then it was back home to pick through and clean the dirt and leaves from the berries, so that they would be ready to freeze or to make into jam. The berries would then be brought out at any time of the year to decorate a cake, or we'd have a

dollop of the jam with our breakfast *filmjölk* (a Swedish natural yogurt). We'd add the mushrooms to the gravy that accompanied our Sunday roast or moose stew. My dad would fry up the chantarelles in some butter and we'd eat them on a piece of bread as an evening snack. These are flavors that I really miss, but as a small gesture to try to include some of nature's bounty in my now home, I have had several bags of frozen lingonberries find their way to the UK in my suitcase.

Living from nature is a way to be more sustainable and foraging connects you with a slow-living lifestyle. Because when you forage, you are not in a hurry. You are in contact with nature, going slowly, eyes peeled for things to add to your basket. By going at a slower pace, you breathe more

Picking mushrooms with my dad Arne, my aunt Barbro, and my two brothers, Michael and Anders, making foraging very much a family affair.

calmly, you start to notice the smells and sounds in nature, and you are also focused because you have a goal. One of my main aims in the summer holidays was finding new places to pick wild strawberries (pictured right) and then keeping those spots a secret, only to be whispered to very special people. There was a lot of joy to be had from threading the wild strawberries on a piece of Timothy grass (a plant that's abundant in northern Europe), lying down in a clearing in the woods, with grass and moss as my pillow, watching the clouds float by, and slowly eating the berries one by one.

Another key aspect of practicing self-care through foraging is that you start to develop a sense of gratitude for the bounty that nature offers us. Those moments of gratitude extend into the winter season, when you are able to pick a jam jar off the shelf and use it at a time when berry-picking season feels very far away. You might crumble some herbs you picked and dried into a recipe, or make a tea by pouring hot water over some dried nettle leaves. This way of eating is also better for the environment. By foraging, you have a smaller impact on the planet. If there are mushrooms in the woods, why would you then go to the shop to buy mushrooms in a plastic container, which probably had to travel for miles to the shop or were grown in a greenhouse. In Iceland for example, mushrooms are by far the most common foraged food, and it's estimated that this

country has more than 100 varieties of edible fungi. Berries and mushrooms are generally the most popular things to pick in most Nordic countries, including Iceland. The Icelandic even have a special word for berry picking, *berjamó*, literally meaning "berry moor." Note that if you would like to look for wild mushrooms yourself, always go with an expert, as many varieties of wild mushroom are poisonous.

In Iceland there is also *blóðberg*, Artic thyme, which grows prolifically due to the perfect conditions of the sandy and gravelly soils. *Blóðberg* is a staple in Icelandic cuisine and the purple flowers are used to make tea. The flavor is reminiscent of oregano and it's

not only used for cooking but is thought to have health benefits such as strengthening the heart, cleansing the blood, and regulating your menstrual cycle. Crowberry, also called Artic blackberry or *krækiber*, is another common thing to forage in Iceland and these are often picked for the purpose of making *kvöldsól* (Evening Sun), which is Iceland's only homegrown red wine. Speaking of wine, I can't mention foraging without the fond memory of helping my sister to pick dandelion flowers for my dad's special brew, *maskrosvin* or dandelion wine…well you might have heard about the strict alcohol-buying laws in Sweden. I've never made it since; however, I have made dandelion syrup, which is lovely.

foraging in the city

Of course, foraging is mainly a country pursuit; not everyone has a wood nearby, and you might live in a city and worry about the pollution. However, I live in a city and I have discovered that foraging is indeed possible there too, if you just know what to look for. The thought that nature can only be found outside of cities is not only wrong but can also be damaging. If you pause for a moment on your rush to the bus stop, you'll find that nature is everywhere, even the edible kind. Yes, it takes a bit more knowledge and can be more challenging. I would start with your local park first. Have a look at what you can identify, then you could buy a book about wild plants and join a foraging group. Just behind our house in London, there is a lone plum tree, laden with fruit each year. It's in between the gardens and is probably a remnant from an orchard that was once there. My freezer has several bags of halved plums, ready for a pie.

Another way to forage the "city way" in the fall is to ask online, local groups if anyone has any spare apples or fruit. There are a lot of apples just being left out to rot in gardens because the owner doesn't know what to do with them or doesn't have time to use them to make something. Self-care is a lot about being self-empowered, and what can be better than gathering food and feeding yourself without having to rely on a large supermarket. Now, these might not get you through a hard winter but perhaps that is not the point—rather, it's to show that you can provide for yourself in a practical way.

If you have a small garden, rhubarb (pictured below right) is the most perfect plant to have. You could even grow it in a pot on a balcony, but it will grow bigger in the ground. My parents had several plants of *rabarber* and the stems, as thick as my arm, were used not only to make a pie or crumble, but also by my mom to make several bottles of beautiful pink cordial every year. She would actually freeze them, as then you didn't need to add so much sugar and there would be no risk of the cordial spoiling. My mom would make cordial from lots of different berries and fruit, even apples, but rhubarb gets a special

mention here as it's a very common plant in a Nordic garden. As a child I used to pick the stalks and dip them in sugar to hide the sourness. In Iceland the name *röllasúra* is reminiscent of that tongue-curling tartness because it means "trolls' sour," although the loaned word *rabarbara* is more commonly used. Rhubarb is one of the only native fruits that grows in Faroe Islands where it thrives in the harsh climate and is made into jams, cordials, and syrup.

I find that rhubarb is a bit forgotten in the UK and elsewhere because most people say they don't like it. But try to make some cordial or my favorite, add it to a pie with a layer of meringue on top, and you might think again. It's a plant that can last you all year and the yield is quite high. The leaves are poisonous but can be used as a fabric dye which doesn't need setting (or "fixing" to the fabric) due to the acidity in the plant. You could also try making the Danish *rabarbergrød*, which is a kind of compote eaten with milk or cream. Or as they say in Danish *"rabarbergrød med fløde."* A favorite sentence with every Danish learner.

eating under the open skies

Lena Flaten is a Norwegian now living in the north of Sweden who runs Flammans Skafferi in Jämtland, which offers workshops and cooking events using local and sustainable foods.

They have close relationships with their suppliers such as the butcher, fisherman, and farmer. She says, "When you know where your food comes from you have more respect for it and you won't be wasting the food. Instead you'll be sure to make use of every last morsel." If you have ever grown your own vegetables from seed, then you know how much time and effort it takes and you might be less likely to waste them or throw them away. "When you care for yourself and what you eat and where it comes from, then everyone benefits and we can create a better world for people, nature, and animals," Lena says. She is passionate not only about teaching people the value of knowing where food comes from, but also about how to fill a larder by foraging from nature. As well as foraging for berries and mushrooms, this also includes finding unusual plants such as *kirskål* (ground elder),

Älgört (Meadowsweet), which you can make cordial from, and also *björk löv*, the leaves of the birch tree which can be used for tea.

Spending time in nature through *friluftsliv* (see page 68) is that key component for adopting Nordic self-care practices, and I would say that this goes hand in hand with eating outdoors. In the Nordics this is not something that is left only for those nice, sunny warm days in the summer. Bringing food along on an outing, either as a picnic or cooking it outdoors, is not a special "event" but something quite normal. However, if winter recreation was not part of your upbringing, you might not realize how easy it is to cook and eat outdoors and the benefits this can provide. The practicalities are often what stop us, but here are some handy tips for eating outdoors in all seasons, especially on those cold—and if you are lucky—snowy but sunny days.

Practical outdoor advice

Equipment

♦ Invest in a good thermos flask. Ideally two—one with a wide mouth for storing food in, and one for a hot drink such as spiced apple juice (see recipe on page 61). I quite like the classic Stanley thermos flask. Also bring something to drink from such as a Swedish *kåsa* cup—a short, wide mug that's perfect for using outdoors.

♦ The Nordics have some very clever outdoor cooking equipment. Trangia stoves were invented in Sweden in 1924, are super-light to carry, and allow you to cook a meal and have a cup of tea in the most compact stove you'll ever see. No fire is necessary, as they use methylated spirit for fuel. On a recent ice-skating trip my sister-in-law Cecilia impressed my kids and made a simple outing so much more fun by whipping out a cast-iron frying pan and cooking up some *krabbelurer* (see page 61) over a fire pit next to the lake.

♦ Lena Flaten, who has been teaching the Swedes how to cook outdoors via her segment on a popular Swedish TV show, knows a thing or two about cooking and eating comfortably from a snow drift in arctic temperatures. For adventures where you want to make a fire (see page 80), she says the best tool to have is a pair of sturdy BBQ tongs, for moving the logs as well as moving the food around. Also take some good gloves—Lena recommends "Those hard wearing workman gloves you can get in a DIY store…or even a pair of wool gloves will protect you briefly from the fire."

Cooking and eating outdoors

♦ Lena says that "Soup is great to bring along in your rucksack as it's both quick and warming on a cold winter's day." Being out on a hike in the fresh air makes you hungry, so don't bring along something that will take too long to cook. "For this reason, make sure you have some snacks you can eat straight away while you cook, such as some soup, dried fruit or meat, especially if there are kids with you as hungry children are not happy children," Lena says.

♦ My personal favorite easy campfire meal is to heat up some Frankfurters in water, then add them to a flask and fill it with hot water, to keep them warm. Then all you need are some hot dog buns, ketchup, and mustard. This is also a very easy thing to do in the Trangia stove, and you can make a cup of tea or coffee at the same time.

♦ Having a jar of porridge oats mixed with dried fruit, nuts, and seeds and a pinch of salt is handy as you only need to add hot water. Salted butter is good to bring as it lasts longer outside the fridge and the salt is good for you if you are out on a longer hike.

♦ Small luxuries such as proper coffee can be so much more enjoyable when you are out in nature and especially after a long walk. Just bring a pour-over coffee cone that can hold a coffee filter. Bring hot water in a thermos flask so you don't have to wait.

♦ Cooking bread over the fire feels like a top-level achievement and we all know how delicious warm, freshly cooked bread is. One of the first things I cooked over an open fire was bread on a stick—*pinnbröd*, or *snobrød*, which means snow bread in Danish. This is very easy to prepare ahead of your hike (see recipe on page 60). The dough keeps well in a plastic bag and you pull pieces from it and roll them around a stick to cook over the fire. Similarly, *gáhkku*—a flatbread recipe from the Sami (the nomadic people of Scandinavia) is also cooked in a frying pan. It is generally made with flour, yeast, syrup, salt, and water but everyone has their own version. It was traditionally served with *suovas* (salted and smoked reindeer) as well as butter and cheese.

♦ Pancake batter, which you can bring with you in a bottle, is pretty quick to whip out and cook over an open fire (see recipe on page 61). *Kolbulle* is another brilliant thing to cook outdoors. It literally means "coal bun" and in the past this was food for lumberjacks, as it's filling and gives lots of energy, and was cooked over charcoal burners. My other sister-in-law, Karin, is

pretty nifty with a hot pan over an open fire and she introduced me to it. The batter is a mixture of flour, water, and salt, which should preferably be made up in advance. Then you fry smoked chopped pork or bacon in a hot pan and pour the mixture over. Once it's cooked you have a delicious, salty, crispy pancake. Now, if that doesn't make you want to make up a fire and go for a picnic outside, I don't know what will.

campfire recipes

PINNBRÖD

14oz (400g) strong white bread flour

½ tsp salt

1½ tsp baking powder

6fl oz (175ml) water

jam, butter, or honey, to serve

Makes about 6

TIP You could also add some grated cheese and/or herbs to the bread mix.

Mix the ingredients together to form a smooth dough, which you can place in a container or plastic bag to bring on a picnic.

Tear small pieces off the dough, roll them into sausage-shaped pieces, and twist each around a stick that you can then "bake" gently over a fire. Turn them so they bake evenly. They are done when you can easily pull the bread off the stick. You could also roll them around a hot dog and grill them like that. They can also be fried in a large frying pan, ideally rolled around a BBQ stick.

Once you have removed the stick fill the hole with jam, butter, or honey.

SPICED APPLE JUICE

4 cups (960ml) apple juice

1 cup (240ml) water

½ cup (120g) brown sugar

1 stick cinnamon, plus extra to serve (optional)

¼ tsp freshly ground nutmeg

½ lemon, thinly sliced, to garnish

½ orange, thinly sliced, to garnish

2 star anise and/or 2 cloves per serving, to garnish (optional)

Serves 4–6

Mix the apple juice, water, brown sugar, cinnamon, and freshly ground nutmeg in a large saucepan and bring to the boil. Turn down the heat and simmer and reduce for about 10 minutes. For a grown-up version you could add a glug of rum or whiskey.

Strain in a sieve and serve in mugs. Garnish with the lemon and orange slices, cinnamon sticks if using, and the star anise or cloves.

KRABBELURER

3 eggs

3½oz (100g) superfine (caster) sugar

18oz (500g) all-purpose (plain) flour

1½ tsp baking powder

pinch of salt

18fl oz (500ml) milk

3 tbsp butter

jam, icing sugar, or superfine (caster) sugar, to serve

Makes about 12–14

In a large mixing bowl, whisk the eggs and sugar together until you get a fluffy mixture. Add the flour, baking powder, and salt, and mix gently to create a smooth batter.

Melt the butter on a medium heat. Drop a tablespoon of batter for each pancake into the pan. Fry and flip once until they are cooked through and doughy in the middle. They burn easily, so watch them carefully. Serve with jam, a dusting of icing sugar, or superfine (caster) sugar.

chapter 3

nature and forest

The outdoor life is deeply rooted in the Nordic soul, and the people of these countries have long lived in tandem with their environment. The Nordic countries often conjure up images of clean, untouched, and undisturbed natural landscapes with few people—the deep forests and lakes of Sweden and Finland, the windswept beaches of Denmark and Åland, and the rugged mountains of Iceland, the Faroe Islands, and Norway.

It doesn't come as a surprise that a love of spending time outdoors is one of the things that the Nordics have in common. The saying "there is no bad weather, only bad clothing" is a maxim all Nordics live by, because if they were worried about a bit of rain, snow, and cold then they wouldn't go out for about six months of the year. Not being preoccupied by the weather can be very liberating—you just get dressed for the occasion and get out. The Nordics know that spending time in nature is beneficial on so many levels, so there really isn't a debate about if the weather fits an outing or not. "It's all about the mindset and it doesn't take much to shift your thinking about weather," says Kari Leibowitz, a PhD student at Stanford University who spent a year in Tromsø, north of the Artic Circle. She discovered that the Norwegians had "a positive winter mindset," embracing the

dark season and turning it into something *koseligt* (providing a feeling of coziness, warmth, and contentment—see page 105).

The Swedish-American writer Linda Åkesson McGurk, author of the book *Open Air Life*, says that when you have spent a large part of your day inside there is a fundamental need to get out of the house. "*Nu måste vi komma ut*" is another mantra I grew up with and means simply that you just have to get outside; it's a way to reset your mood and stops your thoughts from going into overdrive.

Spending time in nature is a big component of creating a self-care routine. Research has shown over and over again how spending time in natural surroundings impacts our mood, reduces our stress levels, and can improve how your nervous and immune systems as well as endocrine system (which is made up of glands that

produce hormones) are working. Studies show that even a single plant in an office, hospital, or school can have a significant beneficial impact, and research from Helsinki University found that kids who swapped gravel and concrete to play on a forest-based playground improved their immunity in only a week. Children playing outside generally fight less, have fewer tantrums, and usually cooperate well.

Deep down we know that connecting with nature is good for us, but if this is not something we grew up with, we might not actively choose it. The Nordics have a long tradition of outdoor childcare provisions, and outdoor time is part of the curriculum in these countries. Norway has several outdoor kindergartens or *Friluftsbarnehager*, and in Sweden, *Skogsmulle* (a method of teaching through outdoor learning activities) has provided nature-based education for children since the 1950s.

When you grow up being used to playing outdoors every day, making "food" from mud and leaves and then later, when you're older, hanging with your friends in the same woods, there will always be something deep in you yearning to get into nature. My dad also taught me the names of plants and flowers, which plants I could eat, and which mushrooms to avoid. Having this knowledge also gives you a deep connection to the outdoors. All the Nordic countries have stories of mythical creatures such as elves and trolls, which are told to children from an early age, giving them a respect and pride in their environment as well as a desire to protect the natural world.

There is something in nature that resonates with humans, making us feel calm and as though we are coming home. This could be explained by how we are part of nature, not separate from it like the philosopher Descartes suggested. Forest bathing, or *shinrin yoku*, is a concept that emerged in Japan in 1908 and means being in the forest, breathing deeply, and taking in the atmosphere. Lots of studies have demonstrated the benefits of forest bathing, including lowering cortisol and blood pressure, and also reducing anxiety. This has given rise to practices such as forest medicine and "eco therapy" (which involves doing activities in nature). Forest bathing is the science of using nature to heal yourself. The Nordics don't need a term like *shinrin yoku* to back up what they have known forever: that being in nature makes you feel better.

friluftsliv (free open-air life)

A concept and a way of living that exists in all Nordic countries, *friluftsliv* translated directly basically means "free open-air life."

The phrase is widely used by the Swedes, Norwegians, and Danes. The Finns say *taivasalla*, which means "under the sky." The term *friluftsliv* was popularized in the 1850s by the Norwegian playwright and poet, Henrik Ibsen, who used it in a poem to explain the experience of being immersed in nature and how that is related to a person's spiritual and physical growth.

This term is used to explain anything from a brisk walk out in the woods to a full hiking trip in the mountains, or joining friends at a lakeside sauna for an after-work steam and swim. The term *friluftsliv* is also linked to the right to roam—*allmansrätten* in Swedish and *friluftsloven* in Norwegian. In Finland you have *jokamiehen oikeudet*—everyman's right, although the right to roam doesn't exist in the same way in Denmark due to population density. How can *friluftsliv* and spending time outdoors support your well-being and help with your self-care? First and foremost, we need to learn to slow down and being in nature has this effect on us, helping us to breathe and move

more slowly. When we shift our attention to nature, we shift it away from our own stresses. By being part of nature, we connect with the cycles of the seasons, which can also bring a sense of calm and inner peace.

The Nordics arrange their lives and activities in a way that gets them outside, through activities such as skiing, swimming, outdoor eating, fishing, and foraging. In Norway, it's not unusual to go for a hike or a bike ride on a first date and in Sweden, many companies incentivise their staff to spend time outside during working hours and block out periods in their calendars to allow them to do so. Studies show that there is both a genetic and environmental component to needing time in nature, so the more you do, the more you create a need for it. The daily practice of seeking out nature where you are is more important than doing a wild trek once a year. Åkesson McGurk (see page 64) says that "setting an intention to get out in nature is key to actually finding a practice which then becomes part of the fabric of your life."

Remember that *friluftsliv* is not connected to a specific activity—you don't need to strap on your skis or travel to a remote area. Instead, taking a daily walk in your nearby city park can be one way of including *friluftsliv* in your self-care practice. It is not about competition and achievement, it's more about choosing nature to be part of your life. You go from a state of doing to a state of just being. The Norwegian tourist board says "it's a commitment to spending time outdoors no matter your age or physical condition."

Globally, 56.2 percent of the population now lives in cities, so most of us don't have a nearby mountain to climb or an uninterrupted view of a valley, but we can make the best of the opportunities we have. I have a dog now and she makes sure that I get out at least once or twice a day to walk her in my local park, and at weekends we sometimes take trips farther away. Living in a city, it is even more important to seek out nature and find out about nearby parks and woodlands. Scientists at the Karolinska Institute in Sweden have found that people who live in cities with plenty of greenery get less sick than those who live in parts of a city with more concrete than vegetation. They also have a lower risk of heart disease and high blood pressure, type 2 diabetes, and mental health issues. The Karolinska

♦ **Connect:** Through outdoor activities with others. People are generally more caring in an outdoor environment and learn more about their values the more time they spend outdoors.

♦ **Be active:** Through hiking, cycling, paddling, or just walking.

♦ **Take notice:** Be curious about how nature changes, take the time to identify plants.

♦ **Keep learning:** Try a new activity, learn about the seasons and gain a new skill, such as making a campfire (see page 80).

♦ **Give:** Leave nature the way you found it or better by picking up litter, or be the first person to make morning tea for your friends when you are camping.

Institute's research also shows that people who have access to parks and greenery are less stressed and more able to concentrate. This is especially evident in children.

Synnevåg Løvoll, an associate professor in *Friluftsliv* at Volda University College in Norway, has done several studies on the benefits of time outdoors and its effect on emotional and spiritual well-being. She says that five documented ways to well-being can all be gained through *friluftsliv*:

wild swimming

Growing up in Sweden, I learned to swim in the summer holidays by going to a swimming school that was held for six weeks at my local lake, come rain or shine.

This was the one chance to learn to swim and each year I improved, I earned metal badges, which were pinned up on a board at home. I still remember cycling to the lake in the summer rain, and because the school began at the end of June, the lake hadn't quite warmed up yet so it was common to swim in water that was 60–65°F (15–18°C). I felt as though I had really earned my badges. I didn't know it at the time, but many of those lessons could probably be categorized as cold-water therapy; even though I didn't have to knock a hole in the ice, it certainly felt like that some days. Each session was always followed by hot chocolate and a cheese sandwich.

Wild swimming, especially in the winter months, is a trend that has been growing in the last few years, particularly following the pandemic. Of course, there have always been hard-core "winter swimmers" or those who like to take a dip in the sea on New Year's Day, but wild swimming in cold water is slowly becoming more mainstream outside of the Nordic countries. Although

no one in the Nordic countries would ever call it "wild" swimming—to us, it's just swimming. The Nordics have always had a tradition of swimming outdoors, whether the water is cold or not, and the health benefits of this practice are numerous.

As well as getting me out from under my mom's feet and learning resilience, the benefits I experienced from being outside, swimming through clean and fresh water, were plenty. Many people who start cold-water therapy as it's also called, report improved mood, stamina, a stronger immune system, and find they don't get so sick in the winter. Another positive effect of cold-water swimming is better sleep, which is of course directly related to improved mood and immunity. There is plenty of scientific research that backs up all of these findings and proves that swimming in open waters, in temperatures of about 14–32°F (-10–0°C) is good for both your physical and mental health.

Greg Whyte, professor of applied sport and exercise science at Liverpool John

Moores University in the UK and a former Olympic pentathlon athlete, explains that the reason open-air swimming is helpful for depression and low mood is that the cold helps your body produce higher doses of dopamine, known as the happy hormone. What is more, wild swimming is often done in a group, so the social aspect can also lift those sad feelings that often occur in the darker and colder seasons.

If you feel that winter and the dark weather is getting you down, wild swimming might help get you through this season and be a self-care practice that lifts you up and empowers you. Of course, you can also try this in the summer and gradually work your way towards swimming in colder temperatures through the fall and winter. If there is one thing that people report after taking their first dip is that they feel elated and exhilarated—even euphoric. And who doesn't want some of that?

Only try wild swimming when you are in good health, and if you don't have any health conditions that would make it unsafe or put extra stress on your body. Here are some tips to help you get started:

1. Wild swimming on your own is not recommended—make sure that you never go alone. It's a good idea to join a local outdoor swimming group, as they will know the best and safest places to swim.

2. Try to get warm from the inside out before swimming. You could do this with a hot drink, which ideally you'd bring along in a thermos flask. A brisk walk to the water is also a good way to warm up effectively. A sauna doesn't work so well as it only warms you up from the outside.

3. Lay out your towel and clothes in the order you need them when you get out of the water.

4. Go slowly into the water—don't run.

5. Wear a woolly hat and don't dip your head in the water.

6. The body's response when we are exposed to the cold is to take a deep breath in, so focus on your breathing and exhale slowly.

7. Keep an eye on the time, and don't stay too long even though you might start to enjoy it after a while. You could start with just 10 seconds, building up to a maximum of three minutes.

8. As soon as you get out, have a hot drink. Get out of your wet clothes quickly, dry yourself thoroughly, and change into warm, dry ones. Wait until you have fully warmed up before taking a warm shower.

Regular cold swimming not only increases the health benefits, but the body's acclimatisation to the cold also helps to protect against hypothermia. Signs of hypothermia are shivering, starting often in the back and chest and affecting your breathing. Other symptoms can be dizziness, nausea, inability to speak clearly, and lack of control over your muscles.

Everyone experiences the "afterdrop," which is a bit of shivering after getting out of the water. This is the body's own defence mechanism to increase its temperature quickly. It's normal, so you just need to break the cycle, get out of your wet clothes, get dry, and into dry clothes. You might also experience a second "afterdrop" when the cold blood from your arms, legs and skin starts to circulate around the central part of your body.

A dip in cold water is not everyone's cup of tea—not even mine as those swimming lessons still feel like yesterday—but what I have learned is that getting out of your comfort zone increases your resilience to stress, and in the end isn't self-care about telling yourself that you are important enough to do things that are good for you.

the importance of good kit

One of my first memories is of me sitting outside on a pile of snow, and because I was wearing scratchy woollen knitted trousers, it was not a happy one.

I seem to remember that this particular garment had been knitted by my *mormor* (grandma). Even though the trousers might have kept me warm and they were a good example of sustainable clothing since they had been worn by all four of my siblings, I didn't much appreciate these finer details and probably cried and wanted to go straight home.

I'm pleased to say that outdoor clothing has moved on since the 1970s, and one thing that this memory taught me is that if you are going to enjoy the outdoors, it really helps to have the right kit. The saying "there is no such thing as bad weather, only bad clothing," comes to mind. If you are uncomfortable or get cold or wet, the great outdoors doesn't seem so great anymore. Considering the weather in the Nordic countries, it's no surprise that they have perfected their outdoor clothes and equipment; some of the best hiking and

outdoor brands are from this part of the world. It's important to bear in mind that having lots of expensive outdoor gear won't necessarily bring you closer to nature, so my advice is to keep it simple but still sensible. Don't forget to look for some of your kit second hand, because there will always be someone who is keen to sell their existing items and upgrade.

Self-care is all about making sure you allow yourself the comfort that fits with your life. Investing in versatile and good-quality basics when it comes to both clothes and equipment is a way of making sure you'll get out outdoors to do that hike again. You'll want to use the layering technique overleaf so loved by the Nordics, as it will help you adjust to your activity levels and whatever the weather throws at you. This might all sound self-explanatory, but many hikes and rambles in the countryside have been ruined by poor

choices of clothes that aren't suitable for
the weather or the ground you're walking
on. By investing in good kit and building it
up slowly, you are telling yourself that you
are committed to getting out in all weathers.
There is self-care in picking the right
winter hat.

think three layers

The **base layer** is all about moisture control—you want a top (as well as a base-layer pair of thermal trousers or leggings for the winter) that dries quickly and wicks moisture away from the skin. Choose either a synthetic material or merino wool. Synthetic dries quickly, is economical to buy and can withstand wear and tear. I've used my Craft base layers for at least two decades and they're still going strong. Merino wool is brilliant as it's multi season—it keeps you warm when it's cold and vice versa. It's also environmentally

friendly and odor-resistant, but it can be expensive and moths love it. A blend of the two is a good choice.

Next up would be your **reinforcement layer**, which is usually a long-sleeved sweater made from fleece or a merino-wool blend. A T-shirt worn over the base layer, with a flannel shirt on top, is usually my go-to combo, and I carry an extra-thin wool sweater in my rucksack. Pair with some comfortable hiking trousers.

Depending on the season, your **waterproof layer** in winter should be a jacket with a generous hood and pockets. It can get warm hiking, so large pockets are handy to pop your gloves and scarves in when the temperature rises. A fleece jacket can be enough in the warmer seasons.

shoes and accessories

If you are into longer treks, your most important purchase will be your shoes, because no one wants to think about sore and uncomfortable feet. Your shoes or boots should be waterproof, so made from Gore-Tex or a thick leather with a good grip on the sole. I think it's also worth buying socks that are meant for hiking as they have the right grip.

Other essentials are of course gloves, hats, and scarves. I like Thinsulated or fleece gloves and a comfortable and non-itchy hat that is fleece-lined. It's quite surprising how hard it is to find a well-fitting hat that doesn't make you look like a dork! Then add a thin cotton muslin or scarf around your neck, and layer a scarf on top to protect your neck and face.

outdoor skills

Spending time in nature is a sure way to use your own body, building up your strength and resilience by getting out in all weathers.

Learning skills that can be used while you're out and about in nature and forests can be powerful as self-care, as they help you to enjoy the outdoors. They can also be a way of building your confidence—for example, if you know how to make up a fire, you'll be able to stay warm and safe and cook your own food. The Swedish society for Nature Conservation has simple instructions on how to make up a fire outdoors (see also right). Always ask the landowner first, and find out whether there is a ban on fires outdoors.

Making a fire

If you haven't brought some firewood, gather some from the ground and make sure that the sticks are dry by listening out for a crack when you break them. Keep the fire away from trees and roots, and protect the ground with a layer of stones. Then build the fire with smaller sticks, dry pinecones, and grass, and light those first. Carefully add thicker pieces of wood. A fire needs dry wood, oxygen, and heat so if you have those three, you will have fire in no time. A good tool which ensures you will always be able to light a fire is a Swedish fire steel—a fire starter developed for the Swedish army. If you want to try some cooking on the go, turn to pages 58–61 for tips and recipes.

how to bring more nature into your life

In a world that is so busy all the time and all about doing, having appointments and meetings, socializing, scrolling social media, and answering messages, it can be so difficult to make time for what actually feels good.

Quite often we can feel confused about what makes us happy and content. Self-care is a lot about setting boundaries in your life and guarding your own time and space. But when society is all about DOING, just BEING can be incredibly hard. Spending time in nature without a goal or a purpose can feel like you are wasting your time, because we are so used to always achieving something. This is where the concept of *friluftsliv* (see page 68) is so brilliant, because it's about connecting with nature in a way that is mindful but isn't necessarily about a particular activity. As Kari Leibowitz (see page 64) explains, "Life is a series of small moments and by giving some of these moments a label, we're using language to set our intentions, make getting outdoors deliberate, and justify the time we spend."

If you find it impossible to see how you could incorporate getting out in nature

on a daily or weekly basis, think about how you could change your schedule to allow yourself to spend more time outside. Perhaps start the morning with a commitment to having your tea or coffee outside. Start to nurture more plants in your house and perhaps offer to walk your neighbour's dog regularly. Synnevåg Løvoll (see page 70) suggests "making a habit of your everyday contact with nature by arranging a walk with a friend. Perhaps study a map of your local area to discover new green spaces. Take your dinner and have it at your local park."

Your intention has to be there to motivate you, so think about how you want to feel and then trust that recognizing the beauty of mother nature will allow your frazzled brain to take a break from life's pressures and simply connect with yourself and your loved ones. Løvoll says that "there

is constant activity in nature, that you only
notice if you sit down and watch. Observing
this activity can be as rewarding as an
experience in itself."

chapter 4

the home and seasonal living

Creating a home that you harmonize with, where you can rest and recharge, is a key way to support your health and well-being. Your home is a reflection of you, and it should be just how you like it without being a slave to what other people think.

Having lived in the UK for many years now, I never think that my home looks particularly Nordic, but people often comment that it has that Scandinavian feel to it. Maybe it's the fabrics, the sanded and oiled floorboards, lots of plants in every window, and of course plenty of small lamps and candles. I've actually lived abroad for longer than I have lived in Sweden now, but there are definitely core values that I grew up with that make me want to arrange my house in a certain way. Even though my home is now a mix of all the countries I've lived in, it has got that essential Nordic touch. This chapter looks at how you can create a home that supports your own self-care, and what the Nordic way of life can teach us about it.

how to nordify your home

You can incorporate some of the key features of the Nordic home into your own, even if you live in a high-rise apartment block in Chicago, a bungalow in Belgium, or a semi-detached 1930s house in southeast London, UK.

The last one is me, by the way. More and more people are relying on their homes to be their sanctuary. Optimizing your house to become a safe space where you can disconnect from the news, politics, and all the craziness in the world, is not only a good idea but a necessity. The first thing you should ask yourself when it comes to changing things in your home is what makes you feel good. There is a level of "optimum stimulation;" when a house or a room becomes too stimulating, our stress levels go up. You need to find that sweet spot where you feel at your most comfortable.

But let's start with the basics and look at exactly what Nordic style is. It emerged in the 1950s as a part of the modern movement in Nordic design that prioritized function and affordability over opulence and luxury. Its characteristics include natural materials, pale colors and

wood, large windows to let as much light in as possible, slim features on furniture such as tapered legs on chairs, and simple lines that leave plenty of open space for an uncluttered and calm look. Maximizing light is very important in Nordic homes, so you won't see heavy curtains covering the windows—instead very light or no curtains. Sunlight is key to well-being; research has shown that natural light exposure in hospitals leads to patients needing less pain medication, and staff reporting feeling happier and more energetic. So maybe drop those heavy drapes.

Not having clutter is key, as it would ruin the clean lines of Nordic design and is a major block to creating a relaxing home. Studies from both UCLA and Princeton show that clutter raises our cortisol levels and impedes our ability to problem-solve. Clever storage solutions are a priority— ideally use textured items such as wicker or wire baskets to add a natural feel. The curious Swedish phenomenon of *döstädning* (death cleaning) comes in here, because it focuses your mind and gives you the motivation to declutter, little by little (see page 106).

One of the core principles of Nordic decorating is creating a feeling of warmth, simplicity, and coziness. The recent popularity of the Danish concept of *hygge* can't have escaped most people, and it has been used to sell candles and blankets, but *hygge* is more about how to create an atmosphere that is easy to relax in. Many Nordic homes have a feeling of comfort without being overly ornate or cluttered, and incorporate just the right amount of furniture and décor. To use that other popularized Swedish word, they are *lagom*, meaning they have just the right amount of stuff—not too much, not too little.

Regardless of their country of origin, using nature as a feature in decorating is a key element in Nordic homes. In houses in all the Nordic countries, you will find natural colors, along with some black and white elements that reflect contrasts in nature. Other key features are natural elements such as wool, wood, and lots of plants, as well as plant designs on textiles and in the art on the walls.

In the early 1930s, the Austrian Josef Frank joined Svenskt Tenn, a Swedish design company founded by Estrid Ericson in 1924. Frank's designs were very influential on Nordic interiors and especially helped to shape Swedish design. Thommy Bindefeld, senior advisor at Svenskt Tenn says, "Josef Frank wanted to put the human in the center of the home, making interiors both beautiful and personable... Frank created botanical patterns that were almost magical in their design with scenes of flora and fauna helping to soften the functional aspect of interiors in Sweden." Josef Frank's style of layering the minimal home with colors and patterns created both warmth and comfort, or *mys*. As Estrid Ericson says, "The simplicity of the room—the richness of detail" is a good benchmark when trying to decorate in a more Nordic style.

Taking some ideas from the Nordic esthetic, here are a few pointers to help you streamline your décor and create your own home sanctuary.

♦ Focus on clean lines and simple, light-colored furniture.

♦ Remove or store away clutter.

♦ Think about sustainability—save up for a good piece of furniture rather than getting a mass-produced piece that might not last as long. Shopping vintage and second hand is one way to give a longer life to furniture.

♦ Incorporate natural materials and bring the outside in. Collect shells, smooth rocks, branches, and pinecones as they will bring back memories from windswept beaches and peaceful forests.

♦ Use plants and flowers, or even just some greenery from the outside.

♦ Less is more, or *lagom* as the Swedes say. Don't overdo the ornaments.

♦ Focus on functionality and practicality.

♦ Think about home accessories that can create that *hygge* feeling. This could be anything that generates a cozy atmosphere and makes an ordinary moment more special, such as lighting a candle as you eat your breakfast in the winter.

living with the seasons

Being so far north of the equator, there are very clear seasons accompanied by changes in the weather and temperature in the Nordic countries, and all of this is reflected in their homes.

We all know that Nordic winters can be harsh, but what some people might not realize is how dark it is in the fall and winter. In Oslo, Norway, the sun rises around 9am and sets at about 3pm in mid-winter. Even farther north, there are only a few hours of daylight, when the light more resembles dusk. The Norwegians even have a word for

this time—*mørketiden* (the dark time)—which perfectly sums it up. The transition of the seasons can bring up emotions and increase stress levels, but using nature as a guide to help you adapt can help to lower anxiety. When you adjust to the seasons, you tune in to yourself and exactly how you are feeling.

The Nordics, perhaps out of necessity, have created some key rituals around the changes of the seasons. They know how to create a home that is supportive to changes in the weather and light. Making your home *koselig* (Norwegian for cozy) is a priority, as so much time is spent at home in response to the long winter and the short days. Thommy Bindefeld, Senior Advisor at Svenskt Tenn says that "Nordics take a lot of inspiration from nature, and because of the weather, we spend a lot of time at home, and also entertain at home, which explains the importance of creating a comfortable and warm environment." As well as adapting to the harsh, cold seasons, the Nordics also make sure to celebrate the long summer nights. On the following pages you will find ways to adjust your home according to the seasons, taking inspiration from the Nordics.

winter

The long Nordic winter season is punctuated by lots of opportunities to get creative in the kitchen, making things to share with family and friends. The highlight in the winter calendar is of course Christmas. However, we can adopt some Nordic habits of making all of the cold and dark season a reason to gather together, eat seasonal and special foods, and make our homes as warm and bright as the outside is dark and cold.

advent

Advent begins on the fourth Sunday before Christmas and marks the official start of the festive season. The Nordic countries have a lot of traditions around Advent, mostly involving decorating the house with candles, stars, and greenery. It is when things start getting magical, with lights shining through the winter darkness, concerts and celebrations, and festive spirits. Advent is then celebrated each Sunday until Christmas Eve.

However, unless you're a churchgoer, Advent in most countries isn't really observed outside of the store-bought chocolate Advent calendar. To introduce a small change in your home to mark the beginning of the season, try baking something that smells delicious and warming yourself up with that first mulled wine of the year. Celebrating in this way can have a huge impact on your mood and actually be an act of self-care.

Let's be honest, November can drag out as it doesn't have much seasonal celebration to look forward to. The most noticeable change is that in many countries the evenings start earlier. Even though it

happens at the same time each year, that blanket of darkness seems to "arrive" out of nowhere, almost by surprise. Advent can be a like a long sigh of relief that we have made it through, and it sometimes begins at the end of November, bringing joy to an otherwise gray month.

Here are three easy ways that you can create some Nordic cheer in the darkest of seasons.

Candles

Get a set of four advent candles (see page 102) and light the first of four candles on the fourth Sunday before Christmas. Candles are usually white but in Norway they are traditionally purple. Then light the candle a little bit each day that week, preferably as you are having your morning tea. Light a new candle each Sunday before Christmas, so that by Christmas Eve all four candles are lit. It's traditional to dress your candle holders with some greenery—you could use moss, branches of pine, and small pinecones. Alternatively, you could use a single advent candle that has all the dates leading up to Christmas on it, which you light a tiny bit each day as a countdown to the 24th.

Fika

Invite your friends to an Advent *fika* (see page 48), and serve some home-baked gingerbread, a Swedish *lussebulle* (a sweet saffron bun), or as they do in Denmark, *aebleskiver*, which is a spherical round

pancake. You don't need a reason to have your friends over for a *fika*, but seasonal treats are a lovely way to enjoy Christmassy flavors such as cinnamon, cardamom, cloves, and ginger. As well as coffee to drink you could also make some piping hot mulled wine—*glögg* in Swedish and Icelandic, *gløgg* in Danish and Norwegian, or *glögi* in Finnish (see page 39).

Window decorations

Decorating your windows with a traditional electric seven-arm advent light is one way to create that warm and cozy, or as the Swedes would say *mysig*, atmosphere.

Seeing the lights in the window can also bring cheer to passersby. A string of fairy lights or a hanging star made from paper, straw, or metal with a light in it would also brighten up an otherwise dark window. The Nordics traditionally hang star decorations in their windows, perhaps because we feel close to the stars during the long winter nights. Because of the low wattage in electric advent lights, I leave them on all night. Having a warm glowing light to greet you makes getting out of bed just that little bit easier.

christmas

Christmas is the brightest shining star in the Nordic winter calendar. Many of the Nordics celebrate it in a similar way, although there are variations from country to country. For example, most Nordic countries celebrate on 24th December and have one Santa bringing the presents but in Iceland, they have 13 *Jólasveinar* (Yule lads) instead. They start delivering little gifts to children from the 12th up to *Jól* (Christmas Eve) on the 24th December.

Throughout the Nordic countries, the festive season starts with Advent, and leading up to Christmas, homes get increasingly more decorated with lots of natural materials that not only give a beautiful scent, but also add a lovely element to the décor.

You could do what the Finns do and celebrate a mini Christmas *pikkujoulu*, an informal party held in the run-up to the 25th. This is when Christmas dishes are brought out for the first time and people generally get together and have a good time.

In Åland, Finland, *Lillajul* is celebrated on the Saturday before the first day of advent. This is when a mini Christmas tree is decorated and there might even be some small gifts under the tree.

Lucia is celebrated on the 13th December in all Nordic countries. It's an atmospheric event where a line-up of people, mostly female, dressed in white and holding candles, come singing and bringing treats to places such as schools, churches, and offices. Each procession is led by one maiden, the Lucia, who carries a candlelit wreath in her hair. This tradition is particular to the Nordics, who use it as a reminder to stop and embrace the dark winter season, as well as an opportunity to light yet more candles. Originally known as *Lussinatta*, after the curious mythical creature *Lussi*, it was introduced in Norway by King Olav in 1020. It's held on 13th December because this was the original winter solstice (the longest night of the year) according to the Julian calendar used at that time. Traditionally in Sweden, staying awake on this night to ward off evil spirits was paramount to safety, and eating helped people to do this. To this day, there is always a bit of a feast attached to a *Lucia* celebration.

We can all agree that Christmas is not meant to be about the presents—instead it's about being together, eating special and seasonal foods, relaxing at home, maybe watching those Christmas movies you have seen many times already, and having days stretched ahead without any plans. Well, that is the idea, but we all know that things don't always turn out that way, and sometimes just the thought of Christmas can make us feel stressed and overwhelmed. So how can we practice self-care during this season?

One suggestion is to start earlier and follow the Nordic tradition of seeing Christmas as not just one day but several small moments and celebrations. Try adding in something festive here and there, such as foods with traditional and warming spices and flavors. Rather than "decking the halls," preferably avoid buying new things and instead reuse the same decorations year after year, only adding more if you pick up something new on your travels or at a market, or if you have kids bringing home crafts from school. Don't get carried away by all the in-your-face commercialism displayed by supermarkets and big shops. Focus on simplicity and natural decorations, scents, and flavors.

Here are some quick tips to help you embrace the winter and festive season in your home.

Winter flowers

Buy and plant traditional winter bulbs in pots in early to mid-winter, so that by the time the darkest season rolls around they are out in bloom and make your house smell amazing. I like using hyacinths, amaryllis, and paperwhites. Once in bloom, water the amaryllis and hyacinth sparsely and keep them somewhere cool at night to prolong the flowering. You can keep the amaryllis as a house plant all year round; stop watering and feeding for about eight weeks in fall, and then repot it for another Christmas.

Once the hyacinths have bloomed, cut the flower stalks off, keep the bulbs somewhere dry, and then plant them out in a flower bed in spring. Paperwhites, from the Narcissus family, are incredibly easy to grow. Add a layer of small stones to a shallow non-draining bowl. On top, layer the bulbs pointy side up and tightly together, add another layer of stones or compost, and then add water. They have a strong scent, and some people can find this overpowering. Personally I find them essential at Christmas.

Simple seasonal crafts

I admit that in my family our crafts end up looking quite homemade, but the point is in the making, in my opinion. So if you are in the mood for some *julpyssel* (Swedish for Christmas crafting), here are a few simple ideas.

♦ **Festive candles:** take some small offcuts of pine from your Christmas tree. Place them on the outside of an empty glass jar and attach them with some rustic twine or a red or white ribbon. Place a tea light in the jar. For a simple hand-made scented candle project, turn to page 102.

♦ **Citrus ornaments:** Cut oranges into slices, place them on a piece of greaseproof paper on a baking tray, and dry them in the oven at 350°F (70°C) for 2–3 hours, making sure you turn them regularly. You could also use limes and lemons to add in some different citrus. Use wire or a needle and thread to string

Cleaning rugs in the snow

I used to think this was just a quirky thing my mom did but no, this is an old tradition which is smart, effective, and environmentally friendly. Make sure that the snow it is dry and not about to melt, and hang your rugs outside so they get cold. Then lay them out on the ground and cover each one with snow. Let them sit for a few minutes, then take a broom and brush off the snow. Repeat on the other side. The smart thing is that the snow absorbs dirt and gives your rugs a newly washed smell.

them up to make a garland, or use them as decorations when wrapping presents.

◆ **Pine decorations:** Use branches of pine to make Christmas wreaths (see page 101), or pop them in a rustic jar as a mini pre-Christmas tree. Ask at a place selling Christmas trees for some offcuts—they usually remove the bottom branches of the trees and will normally give them to you for free. Add some eucalyptus for a more spicy scent. If you are not in the mood or don't have the other materials necessary to make a wreath, just tie the branches together with some sturdy string, add a nice red ribbon, and hang them on the door. The easiest thing for a welcome at the door is to just pop the branches outside the front door as an alternative Christmas doormat.

simple wire wreath

This wreath is very simple so why not make several to hang on doors, outside or inside. For the greenery, you could use pine branches in the winter, flowers and foliage in the summer, or sprigs of fall leaves and berries in the fall.

materials
About 1yd/1m sturdy florist's wire
Greenery
Bells (optional)

tools
Wire snips

1. Decide how large you want your wreath to be, work out the circumference, and cut a piece of wire to that length. Make a circle from your wire and twist the ends together to secure.

2. Cut several lengths of wire about 8in (20cm) long. Thread a couple of jingle bells, if using, onto each piece of wire.

3. Take a piece of greenery, put it on the wire circle, and use the smaller wire with bells on it to secure the greenery to the wire. Keep working all the way around until the wreath is complete.

cinnamon- and orange-scented candles in enamel mugs

Utilitarian-looking enamel mugs can create beautiful candles, and adding cinnamon and orange scents to the wax gives them a deliciously wintery feel. When the wax is molten the mugs will become hot, so make sure that you place them on a suitable surface to avoid scorch marks.

materials
Wick
Wick sustainer
Enamel mug
Wax adhesive
Soy wax
Cinnamon scent and orange scent

tools
Double boiler (or you could use a bowl
  placed over a pan of water to melt the wax)
Thermometer
Wooden spoon
Pitcher (jug)
Scissors
Small pliers
Wooden skewer
Teaspoon

1. Cut a length of wick to the height of the mug, plus about 2in (5cm). Thread the end through a wick sustainer and squeeze the sustainer with pliers to fix it in place.

2. Take a small piece of wax adhesive and use it to stick the wick sustainer and wick inside the mug. Press it down firmly. Tie the end of the wick around a small piece of wooden skewer so that the wick is taut and the skewer rests on the rim of the mug.

3. Melt the soy wax in a double boiler and heat to 140°F (60°C). Add a few drops of orange and cinnamon scent. Stir the scent in gently.

4. Pour the wax into the mug, pouring slowly and smoothly so that it does not splash. Leave the candle to cool completely.

5. If the wax dips in the middle (soy wax doesn't usually dip), then melt a little more wax in the same way and top up the candle. When the wax is hard, slide the skewer out and untie the wick. Trim the wick to about ¾in (2cm).

spring

In this season, the days are getting longer and the worst of the dark, cold weather is over. Spring is one of the shorter seasons but because of the return of the light and longer days, it is something to really celebrate. Nature slowly starts to wake up again, trees are budding, and small shoots of green can be seen everywhere.

This is also the time where you can play "spot a Nordic person" as they will always find a *solglänta* or sunny corner to sit in and get those rays. After a long winter, the sun is very welcome, so never mind that the temperature is low, the Norwegians will wrap up warm to enjoy that first *utepils*

(beer drunk outside) by their log cabin or *hytta*. Perhaps it is the long winter that explains why Norwegians go a bit mad around Easter and see it as a big party of skiing, eating chocolate, and curiously, reading *påskekrim* (crime novels).

Easter in the Nordic countries signals not only longer days but also a long public holiday to spend with family and friends. In Sweden, it is celebrated by decorating with lots of yellow and green colors and adding cut branches, especially from the birch tree, to vases with colorful feathers for a beautiful and simple *påskris* or spring display. In the Nordic countries, Easter for the most part is a perfect combination of secular and religious traditions. In Finland *pääsiäinen* is celebrated by all, and in Denmark, an Easter breakfast or *påskefrokost* is a must. Spring is all about noticing the return of the light and the flower bulbs popping up in gardens and parks. The Nordics love decorating their homes with plants and flowers, and spring is when they can really indulge in their love of tulips.

A 2018 study entitled *The Impact of Flowers on Perceived Stress Among Women* found that adding flowers to indoor environments results in a statistically significant and meaningful reduction in stress. The lead researcher Erin Lago-Wight, Ph.D., Associate professor of the University of North Florida's Department of Public Health says that "When life seems to be in a constant state of frenzy, flowers can provide us with a much-needed moment of calm."

Use these ideas to help you make the most of this season in your home.

Seasonal bulbs

If spring is taking its time, plant some flower bulbs such as pearl hyacinths or daffodils in a pot with soil, cover with moss, and start spring a little earlier indoors.

Tree branches

Cut a few bare tree branches where you are allowed to do this, and add them to a vase filled with water. After few days in the warmth, the branches will start to bud and give you a taste of what is to come in nature.

Tulips

Buy tulips and dot them around your home in small vases. Tulips love very cold water, so change the water often. The tulip is Sweden's most popular flower and the Swedes buy more tulips per capita than even the Dutch.

Spring display

Do as in Finland and create some indoor "grass" by planting rye grass seeds in a shallow dish with some soil. As the grass grows, decorate it with some mini bunnies and chicks, and stick in little branches as small trees. Kids love these little displays.

Table decorations

Decorate your spring or Easter table with a yellow tablecloth and lots of small vases of flowers, and make some displays of marbled eggs. These are very simple to make: wrap some eggs in onion skins, cover them in foil, place them in a pan of water, and bring to a boil. Lower the heat and simmer for 15–20 minutes. Remove the eggs, leave to cool, and then remove the foil and onion skins.

summer

This is when the Nordics throw open their windows and start living outside more to maximize the light and long days. Because of this, they take a lot of care to create a beautiful space outside and curate it in a way that makes them want to spend lots of time there. This is the season that gives us Midsummer, and while all the Nordic countries celebrate the summer solstice (the longest day of the year), the way they recognize it varies. In Denmark, it is linked to the birth of St. John the Baptist, and they call it Sankt Hans Aften. In Finland, Denmark, and Norway, big bonfires are lit. In Sweden it's all about the Maypole—a painted pole that's decorated with flowers, around which people traditionally dance.

As much as the Nordics like to bring nature inside, this is the time of the year where you can really blend the outside with the inside, just by using every moment to hang out outdoors.

decorate your outdoor space

If you have a garden or a space outside, make it into somewhere you'll want to spend as much time as possible. Like the Nordics, decorate your patio, balcony, or garden with beautiful scented flower arrangements, comfortable chairs with blankets to wrap up in when the evenings get cooler, throws and sheepskins on the chairs, lots of outdoor candles, fairy lights, and plastic rugs on the patio.

grow scented flowers

Plant scented flowers near your patio, outdoor space, or balcony if you have one—wherever you like to sit to have your tea in the morning or glass of wine in the evening. Keep it simple by using seeds—it's a small investment with maximum return. Try Nicotiana Sylvestris, also known as the tobacco plant. It can grow up to 4½ foot (1.5m) tall and has a sweet fragrance that comes out in the evening. Also try Cosmos (pictured left), an easy plant to grow, which has a long flowering season.

fall

As the evenings draw in, it's time to start making your home all cozy again. Or as the Norwegians would say *koseligt*, or as the Faroese say *hugnaligt*. Get your candles, blankets, and sheepskins out and create more *mys* (warmth and comfort). This might be the time you start on that knitting project. *Guðrun Rógvadóttir*, one of the founders of the knitwear company Gudrun and Gudrun, and also the creator of the famous sweaters from the Danish TV series *The Killing*, says that knitting is huge in the Faroe Islands: "We spend a lot of time indoors in the colder months so knitting is a way of just being at home whilst also creating something."

Because of the harsh weather, the wool of the sheep from the Faroe Islands is adapted to these conditions. It is rich in natural oils, which makes it water repellant and self-cleaning, hence it is steeped in tradition. "*Ull er føroya gull* wool is the gold of the Faroe islands," says Guðrun Rógvadóttir, who also adds that knitting is a kind of "meditative process, a way of slowing down… We get a lot of orders from Japan and they are not only buying a jumper, they are also buying the idea of the time it took to knit the garment."

Here are some ways that you can adapt to and embrace this season in your home.

Crafting
Start on a simple knitting project, such as a hat (see page 110), dish cloth, or snood—something that you can pick up without having to think a lot about the next step.

Flowers and plants
Make simple fall flower arrangements in your outside space if you have one, and plant things such as ornamental cabbage, heather, and ivy.

Seasonal decorations
Decorate your home with colorful fall leaves and small pumpkins. By using thin branches you can easily make a fall wreath (see page 100). Attach pine cones, sprigs of berries such as Rowan berries, and whatever else remains from the last of the summer, such as leaves, flowers, or seedpods.

Fair Isle pompom hat

If you're new to Fair Isle knitting, this Nordic-look pompom hat is the perfect place to start, because the color changes are close together so there's no stranding.

yarn
Sirdar Cashmere Merino Silk
(75% merino wool, 20% silk, 5% cashmere) light worsted (DK) weight yarn, 127yd (116m) per 1¾oz (50g) ball
    1 ball in each of:
    Orchard Red 416 (A)
    Mother of Pearl 408 (off-white) (B)
(If you wish to substitute a different yarn for the one above, try the Yarnsub website for suggestions: www.yarnsub.com.)

needles and equipment
US 6 (4mm) knitting needles
Yarn sewing needle
A pompom maker to make 2¾in (7cm) pompoms, or two cardboard circles each measuring 2¾in (7cm) in diameter with a 1¼in (3cm) diameter hole in the center.

gauge (tension)
22 sts and 28 rows in stockinette (stocking) stitch to a 4-in (10-cm) square on US 6 (4mm) needles.

measurements
The finished hat measures approx. 16in (40cm) circumference and 8½in (22cm) high.

abbreviations
cont continue
k knit
k2tog knit 2 stitches together
p purl
p2sso pass two slipped stitches over, pass two slipped stitches over another stitch
p2tog purl 2 stitches together
rem remain(ing)
rep repeat
skpo slip one stitch, knit one stitch, pass slipped stitch over knitted one, to decrease
sl2 slip two stitches, from the left-hand needle to the right-hand needle without knitting them
st(s) stitch(es)
[ ] work instructions within brackets as many times as directed

For the hat
Cast on 102 sts in A.
Row 1: [K1, p1] to end.
Rep row 1, 11 times more.
Break A and join in B.
Work 14 rows from chart.
Rep last 14 rows once more.
Rep rows 1–10 of the chart once.
Cont in B only.
Row 51: K1, [skpo, k5] to last 3 sts, skpo, k1. *(87 sts)*
Row 52: Purl.
Row 53: K3, [sl2, k1, p2sso, k3] to end. *(59 sts)*

Row 54: P1, [p2tog] to end. (30 sts)
Row 55: [K2tog] to end. (15 sts)
Row 56: [P2tog] 3 times, p3tog, [p2tog] 3 times. *(7 sts)*
Break yarn, thread it through rem sts, and pull up securely.

to make up

Sew the back seam using mattress stitch.

Using the pompom maker or cardboard circles, make a pompom, winding yarns A and B together.

Tie the pompom using B. Trim the pompom and use the tails of yarn to sew it to the top of the hat.

Weave in all loose ends.

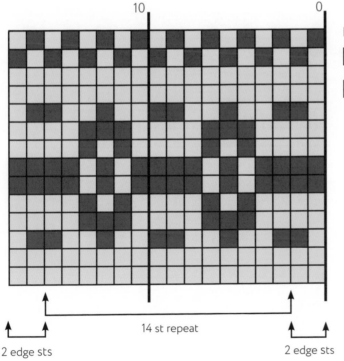

key

Orchard Red 416 (A)

Mother of Pearl 408 (off-white)

10   0

14 st repeat

2 edge sts   2 edge sts

döstädning (the Swedish art of decluttering)

After both her mother and her husband passed away within a short time of each other, Margareta Magnusson had to clear out their things, which she found exhausting and incredibly emotionally taxing. She decided to write a book about the importance of reducing your belongings so your loved ones wouldn't have to go through the same thing after your passing, and coined the process *döstädning* or death cleaning. The book hit a nerve and became a bestseller the world over.

Döstädning is all about downsizing your home and belongings so that life after death can literally be lighter and easier for those who have to clear out your house. At the same time, you make your own daily life much easier, because who doesn't want less clutter? We all have so many things that we have accumulated from who knows where and don't appreciate anymore. If you are over 50, this is especially something you might want to consider doing, because something strange happens when you hit midlife, when all of a sudden you are faced with the realization that life is finite.

However, it doesn't have to be about death or dying, because if you can't shut your drawers or cupboards, it's time do something about it. Death cleaning is about making two piles: one to keep and one to get rid of. It might take a while to declutter, so start adopting this as a habit instead of having one massive clear out. The point of *döstädning* is to imagine someone else having to.clear up your house, a thought that might spur you on to dealing with some of those skeletons in the closet. They might not be "secrets" as such, but perhaps embarrassing items you might want to keep to yourself. We all have a few of those.

One method of *döstädning* is to put things into boxes and label them so that it is clear what to do with them. You might not be ready to get rid of these things yet, but this makes it easier if someone else has to.

A lot of the items we surround ourselves with have memories attached to them. What meaning do they have when they're drowning in drawers, on dusty cluttered shelves, or packed away in a cupboard? Instead, you could pass an item on to someone else who might have more use for it, telling them its story so it can carry on making memories in their house. *Döstädning* is a way of summarizing your life in a practical way and unearthing possessions that spark memories. Be happy about the memories that are attached to your items, and know that you don't need things to

remember the fun stuff. See the act of
döstädning also as an opportunity to invite
your loved ones into a conversation about
what we all avoid talking about—death,
a fate that no one can avoid.

chapter 5

a balanced life: nordic mindfulness

The Nordics have a calm approach to life and take their time to do things right. At work they will set aside tasks to have regular breaks for *fika* (see page 48) together, not alone.

The Norwegians regularly take Friday afternoons off to enjoy their *friluftsliv* (see page 68) and a recent four-day working week trial in Iceland was a big success, showing that productivity stayed the same. The Nordic countries seem to have nailed that elusive goal of a good work–life balance mainly because they have normalized flexible and remote working.

The Nordics also take time to do things they enjoy in an uncomplicated way, and celebrations such as Christmas, Midsummer, and Easter are usually low key with a strong focus on being together with family or friends. When you find a balanced way to do things, they become more manageable and you can take the pressure off yourself and others too. And weirdly, when you take things slow, you actually gain more time.

It's not news that the Nordic countries have their fair share of issues with mental health. However, perhaps because of that they also have a good idea how to solve some of these problems, which are by no means exclusive to the Nordic countries. Each country and culture has their way of dealing with these issues, but what the Nordics have in abundance is their love of the outdoors and a connection to the natural world. After all, humans are a part of nature, so it's no surprise that turning to it can be the answer to a lot of mental health issues facing the world. That is where we can really learn a lot and adopt some of the Nordic mindset in our own lives.

health in nature

Frisk I Naturen, Health in Nature, was a joint project run by the Nordic outdoor organizations between 2009–11 and financed by the Nordic Council of Ministers, NMR, which is the main forum for Nordic co-operation.

The goal was to gather knowledge around what nature and *friluftsliv* can do for health, and put it high on the political agenda and in the hands of decision makers in society. It also aimed to give this knowledge to people working in health and nature sectors, so that they could apply it in their work. The connection between nature and health could then be reinforced by health-care workers, landscape gardeners, and city planners. Almost 80 percent of people in the Nordic countries live in or close to a city, so planning green areas and playgrounds in urban areas is key for allowing opportunities for *friluftsliv*, as well as for making cities more green and nature friendly. The Health in Nature report also aimed to help everyone feel more motivated to involve nature in any way in their everyday lives.

The positive effect nature has on mental health was clear from this extensive report. Research has shown that nature has a calming influence, and that recovery from

a stressful period is very effective if spent in a natural setting. Stress is a major factor in many illnesses such as heart disease, high cholesterol, obesity, and Alzheimer's, to name a few. Just by spending time in nature, you can reduce stress and in turn help to prevent so many of the illnesses we just think are part and parcel of a modern lifestyle. Studies have shown that even a short time of only 4–5 minutes spent in nature is beneficial, which is good to know for city dwellers, so try to find a green area where you can spend time or even just walk through on your way from work.

nature therapy

The "biophilia hypothesis" is the idea that because our ancestors evolved in wild settings and relied on the environment for survival, we have a built-in need to connect with nature that is rooted in our biology and evolution. Humans aren't really built for our modern lifestyle; Homo sapiens have lived on earth for at least 50,000 years and our biology has only changed about 0.003% since the ice age, which lasted until 11,500 years ago. It's not surprising that the speed that characterises today's society has a detrimental effect on our mental health. We are constantly switched on, and every minute of the day is planned with activities where nature simply does not fit in. With most people now being able to work from home, being able to check messages wherever and whenever can also cause quite a lot of stress.

Sweden's largest union, Unionen, reports that while many embrace the freedom of flexible working, rising numbers of members report feeling stressed as they are unable to unwind like they did in the past. This is particularly relevant for entrepreneurs who might not either talk to anyone during the day so don't have that natural "watercooler" break in the day…or *fika* break if you are in Sweden.

As an antidote to this, across the Nordic region, nature or garden therapy for burnout, chronic fatigue, and PTSD is readily available on the health service. At Alnarp University of Agricultural Sciences in Sweden, they have had a rehabilitation or healing garden since 2002, where it has been demonstrated again and again how surrounding yourself with plants can be more effective than using medication. The lead researcher Patrick Grahn, wrote in a paper in 2017 that "As many as 68 percent of the participants returned to work or participated in job training or work-oriented measures, full- or part-time, after one year… Study outcomes indicate that a longer rehabilitation period in a rehabilitation garden increases the possibility of a return to paid work."

hug a tree

The Japanese practice of *shinrin-yoku* (forest bathing) is well known, and it became part of Japan's national health programme in 1982. The Icelandic Forest Service suggested something similar during the lockdown in 2020. They recommended that people go out and hug a tree, even putting up lots of pictures on their website to show people how to do it, and saying that when you hug a tree you can feel it in your toes and feet first, and this feeling then travels upward in your body. I have been called a "tree hugger" in the past, mainly due to my eco-warrior habits, and science now shows us that it's not such a mad idea after all.

Dr. Miles Richardson, a nature

connection psychologist and the author of the book *Reconnected*, says "When we're in the presence of trees, our heart rate changes, calming and rebalancing the systems that regulate our emotions." One Korean study of patients diagnosed with moderate to severe depression compared the effects of CBT (cognitive behavioral therapy) done in a hospital to CBT performed in an arboretum and found that symptoms of depression were most significantly reduced in the forest setting. The patients in the forest setting also experienced a 20–30 percent higher rate of complete remission, compared to the medicated group. Dr. Richardson agrees and says that "Touching trees reinforces the idea that we are at one with nature. That connection, in turn, has been linked to things like greater life expectancy, a higher sense of 'meaningfulness', lower cognitive anxiety and better body image."

One of the things that happens from hugging trees is that the hormone oxytocin, which is responsible for emotional bonding, calmness, and trust, increases in the body. In his book *Blinded by Science*, Matthew Silverstone shows how it's the vibrational properties of trees and plants that offer the health benefits, and when you are touching a tree these different vibrations affect biological behaviors. Silverstone provides plenty of proof that the benefits of tree hugging are not just for hippies but for everyone.

living with light

The Nordic countries place much significance on light. From the endless brightness in summer to the deep darkness in winter, light has become a key part of their culture. Even when the absence of sunlight is most evident, the sky sometimes lights up with the help of the northern lights. You'll know a Nordic person as they will be the ones sitting outside in the winter months, wrapped up warm, perhaps under a heat lamp, with their faces aimed toward the sun as soon as it makes an appearance.

A lot of Nordic buildings are designed and built with a special focus on how to best use the scarce light in winter, as well as the light throughout the long summer days. Adapting to the seasons and having several light spots is important indoors, as well as maximizing the natural light coming in by avoiding covering up windows in winter.

When it comes to our health, low levels of natural light can have implications not only because it reduces the production of vitamin D in our bodies, but also because it affects our sleep-wake cycle, and serotonin and melatonin production. There are vitamin D receptors all over the body, as well as in the heart and reproductive organs, for example—basically in a lot of places where the sun don't shine! Studies show that low levels of vitamin D play a role in SAD (Seasonal Affective Disorder), which is very common in the northernmost countries, and that increased vitamin D status lowers depressive symptoms.

Here are some ways that you can help to increase your levels of vitamin D:

♦ Phototherapy—using a lamp such as the Lumie—has been shown to help significantly with SAD symptoms and the sleep cycle especially. If you'd like to use one, it's important that the lamp is strong enough; 10,000 lux is four times more effective than 2500 lux.

♦ You can take vitamin D supplements, and complement your diet with vitamin K for maximum vitamin D absorption. Also make sure that you have enough cholesterol (saturated fat) in your diet, as it is a carrier for all fat-soluble vitamins including vitamins D and K. Make sure you go to a health practitioner to get advice and check your vitamin D status before supplementing.

♦ The "D-minder" app is also useful if you want to find out how much time you need to spend outdoors to get your correct amount of sunlight, including UVB rays, which stimulate vitamin D production. The app uses your location to work out your solar noon—when the sun is at its highest in the day.

Ultimately, there is no substitute for natural light. A Finnish research group showed that the length of daylight affects the opioid receptors in the body, which regulate mood as well as sociability. And contrary to what you may have heard, sunlight, especially red and infrared light, can be very good for the skin. Early morning sunlight pre-conditions the skin, and the light at sunset repairs it. Trials show that sunset light reduces fine lines, wrinkles, and increases collagen density. It's free, effective, and makes you feel good as well as giving you youthful skin. No more excuses—get out there and get some daily rays.

sisu

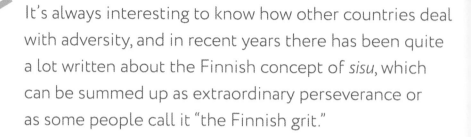

It's always interesting to know how other countries deal with adversity, and in recent years there has been quite a lot written about the Finnish concept of *sisu*, which can be summed up as extraordinary perseverance or as some people call it "the Finnish grit."

Similar but not as well-known is the *þetta reddast* mentality in Iceland, which basically means that things will work out, and to keep going and never give up. Thorgerdur (or *Þorgerður* in the Icelandic spelling) Anna Gunnarsdóttir, Political and Communications Officer at the Icelandic Embassy in London says, "We have survived centuries in that barely inhabitable place so we can do anything. We really believe in ourselves."

You could do worse than applying some *sisu* in your life, because it teaches you how to have a strategy for hard times. Even though no one has taught us how we are genetically and biologically prepared to deal with adversity, the ability to do this is common among all humans. If it was a taught skill, humans wouldn't still be here, as we have got to where we are now through three traits: perseverance, resilience, and courage.

In November, 1939 Russia declared war on Finland. Eight hundred thousand Finnish soldiers had to defend against two million Russian soldiers, and the confrontation between them is one of the most fascinating in history. The Finns resisted stoically, which strengthened this idea of *sisu*; the potential you have inside. The concept of *sisu* historically goes back 500 years or more but nevertheless, this is a good story to describe it.

All humans have this potential dormant inside of them. Adversity awakens it in us, when we use it to resist, overcome, and persist. Some of the lessons you can take from *sisu* are to control stress and not let fear dominate you. Perseverance is a trait in decline as most of us are impatient and want things right now, but as the old saying goes, good things come to those who wait. Learn how to be resilient now and always—it is a sign of someone who is brave and

courageous and who has learned how to deal with life's adversities. You don't brag about it, you let your actions do the talking. However, be mindful and know when to ask for help. Tiina Knuuttiila (see page 22) says, "*sisu* is an integral part of one's self-worth, I must be able to be strong and resilient for that is what I am. But on the flipside it's a sense of duty and independence and not asking for help, because if I do then I owe them and hence is not really free." As well as *sisu*, make sure that you practice simple self-care so you can in turn look after other people too and ask for help yourself.

burnt out in a cold climate

Despite their many holidays, the social "safety net," and the low cost of childcare, a very high number of people in the Nordic countries are being signed off long-term for "burnout" or *utbränd*.

To say that you are *utbränd* is socially accepted in many of these countries, which as a general rule don't display a lot of emotions. Michelle Baker, a New Yorker living in Sweden who teaches yoga and breathwork, says she had never heard of this concept before she arrived in Sweden. She says that "Summers in Sweden are intense, people have lots of time off, but no one makes time for yoga and relaxation and as a result, they come back in the fall totally exhausted and at the point of burn out."

Anja Headicar, a psychotherapist from Denmark who after many years the UK, moved back to her homeland, says this "burn-out phenomenon" has "become socially accepted and that instead of dealing with why you have reached this point, you can deflect and say that your employer has something to do with it." She points out that social mobility is very high in Denmark. In fact, Denmark tops the list of social mobility followed by Norway, Finland, Sweden, and Iceland, partly due to a high level of trust in the government. This also comes with very good health care and a social safety net, so if you can get a diagnosis of burn out, it's official and no explanation is needed.

In contrast, in Finland this doesn't exist as such, says Tanja Luukkanen, Senior advisor for Occupational health at Trade Union Pro, "which leads to the fact that the cause of burnout is not addressed at workplaces, because the cause is considered to be the employee's personal problem and symptoms are often recorded as depression or anxiety."

the law of Jante

Alongside burnout, the use of antidepressants is quite high in the Nordic countries, which might also be to do with the Law of Jante (also known as *Jantelagen* in Swedish, *Janti laki* in Finnish, *Jantelögin* in Iceland, and *Janteloven* in Norwegian and Danish).

This is a widespread social conduct that translates into an emphasis on conformity rather than individuality, and a general disapproval of anyone who stands out from the collective. The advert for Carlsberg saying that "it's the best beer in the world" ending with "probably" pokes fun at this concept, and in 2018 on *The Late Show with Stephen Colbert*, the Swedish actor Alexander Skarsgård explained in a funny way how he really struggled with winning an Emmy because it meant success and recognition. The exception is in sports, where the Nordics love to win over their neighbouring countries, especially in skiing and ice hockey. It can get very personal—no joke.

However, we can't deny that this focus on the collective has helped to shape the success of the Nordic societies. For example, workplaces are designed to be communal and social environments, with shared spaces in offices allowing for more creativity and opportunities for the workers to be seen and heard in their teams. The negative aspect of a collective mindset can be that the individual is pushed aside, leaving people feeling like they are not able to speak and live their truth. It can be hard and painful to break out of your "bubble." You don't need to be Nordic to know that this is not very supportive for good mental health.

how to live more mindfully, the nordic way

Despite all the benefits of the Nordic countries it's clear there are still some things that aren't perfect, but maybe because of this, we can gain wisdom from how the Nordics manage stress and overwhelm. Here are some suggestions to help you stay mindful and sane in an increasingly crazy and busy world.

prioritize taking time out in the day

Make time for small moments of enjoyment to have *fika* or, if you are in Finland, *pullakahvi* (coffee and a bun). If we don't stop, we just keep on going and going. Even something small such as making a hot drink in your favorite mug with some loose-leaf tea and a strainer, rather than just chucking a teabag in a mug with a splash of milk, can make a moment more mindful. Having a favorite corner in your garden or in a natural space near your home, where you can sit and relax during the day without too much fuss, is ideal. You could also find a favorite walk where you can observe nature's changes throughout the year. Many people find that regularly returning to the same place at the same time helps with relaxation. The brain switches to chill mode faster if it knows that you are in a place where you can relax.

seek out the sun, especially in the morning

If you live in northern Europe, getting enough light in the winter months can be difficult, so prioritizing getting enough natural daylight is essential. When we are outside we get a boost of brain-energizing chemicals, particularly in the morning light. By being outside, we also avoid artificial

live seasonally

Allow yourself to "hibernate" during the darker and colder months, and don't push yourself to be sociable and super active if you don't want to be. Spend that time intentionally by making your house as comfortable as possible, adding plants to your windowsill, cooking seasonal comfort foods, knitting some socks, clearing out clutter, and hunkering down in front of a good movie for some *fredagsmys* (cozy Friday nights in). Make more room for the Norwegian *kos*, which is about enjoying the small luxuries in life and which the Norwegian tourist board defines as "the kind of instant happiness you get when you feel safe, warm, and good together... Especially during long and cold winters."

spend more time outdoors

Make a "date" with the outside world regularly, even schedule it in your diary if that is what it takes. Seek out activities that include an outdoor element, such as joining a walking or running group, hiking, foraging, and Nordic walking (a technique that involves walking with poles to work your upper body as well as your legs). Just find something that you enjoy, embrace the weather whatever the season, and practice what Kari Leibowitz calls a "good winter mindset," and if it takes an *utepils* (beer enjoyed outside) to do it, so be it. Getting outdoors is an excellent form of self-care as you always feel better afterwards.

light and its flicker, which can cause issues with your natural circadian rhythm. Carrie Bennett, a clinician and educator in quantum biology says that "Without the changing frequencies of full spectrum light, regardless of whether it is sunny or cloudy, our body starts to become more chaotic." If you are struggling to fit in natural light in the day, consider making some adjustments to your schedule, such as waking up a little earlier so you can expose your face to the sunrise, or taking a regular lunchtime walk.

simplify your life and try to avoid consumerism

Surround yourself with nice things but don't fall into that trap of believing that spending money on stuff makes you happy. We've all been there in Ikea, coming out with another Pärkla storage case instead of decluttering. There is a fine line in between taking up a new hobby and buying an excessive amount of gear for it, so aim for the sensible *lagom* approach here. Focus more on unpretentious moments with friends and family, and creating *hygge* with simple things such as cooking uncomplicated food together or even outdoors, perhaps accompanied by a fire or lots of candles.

practice resilience

Everyone has it in them to overcome hard times. Remember that you are stronger than you think. Remind yourself of how far you have come and all the obstacles you had to get through as proof that you have grit and courage within you. Susanna Heiskanen from the popular lifestyle blog and podcast "The Nordic Mum" says, "I think that is what all Finns if not broadly speaking Nordic people have in common. We come from countries where you have had to fight hard to make your living over centuries on harsh climate and conditions and only the toughest and most resilient people have survived. Something that I want to teach my kids is that *sisu* is inner strength and it will serve you well when times are tough."

resources

health and beauty

Michelle Baker Breathwork and yoga. Michelle is originally from the States. She is based in Sweden but has beautiful online offerings
www.michellebaker.co

Carrie Bennett Quantum Biology Educator and Clinical Nutritionist
www.carriebwellness.com

Divine Saunas Nordic sauna shop in the US
www.divinesaunas.com

Filter Optix A Norwegian company selling blue light-blocking glasses
www.filteroptix.com

Kjaer Weis Organic Danish make-up
www.kjaerweis.com

L:a Bruket Beautiful skincare from a town close to where I grew up in Sweden
www.labruket.com

Neven Norwegian natural skincare brand promoting sustainability and healthy living
www.neven-body-care.com

Nörre Nordic Simple and natural Finnish skincare
www.norrenordic.com

Oura Ring A Smart ring that uses sensors to track various health metrics such as sleep patterns, heart rate, body temperature, and oxygen. Founded in Finland in 2013
www.ouraring.com

Reclamation Organics American skincare made in small batches. Focuses on simple products that support your skin barrier.
www.reclamationorganics.com

Red Light Man All things red and infrared light
www.redlightman.com

Sóley Organics Icelandic skincare
www.soleyorganics.com

Straightforward Nutrition by Linn Thorstensson. Nutrition coaching around disordered eating
www.straightforwardnutrition.com

food

Heimablidni Eat-at-home culinary experience in Faroe Islands, Heimablídni
heimablidni.fo

Scandi kitchen Lovely shop in London and online where you can get your Nordic food fix
www.scandikitchen.com

outdoor gear and equipment

Espegaard Norwegian company for all things outdoor cooking
www.espegard.com

Gudrun & Gudrun Knitwear company from Faroe Islands and the creator of "The Jumper" from the TV series *The Killing*
www.gudrungudrun.com

The Handknitting Association of Iceland Icelandic sweaters and accessories
www.handknitted.is

The Icelandic Store
www.icelandicstore.is

Outnorth Online shop for outdoor clothes and gear
www.outnorth.com

Muurikka Finnish company that makes outdoor cooking equipment from fire pits to waffle irons
www.muurikka.com

Sea & Stream Outdoor swimming gear plus books, art, and lots of information about wild swimming
www.seaandstream.co.uk

wild swimming and the outdoors

Canopy and Stars Glamping and cool camping in the UK
www.canopyandstars.co.uk

Flammans Skafferi Go to the north of Sweden and learn to cook and eat using local ingredients and forage in wild, unspoiled nature
www.flamman.nu

Outdooraholics London Hiking, walking, travel
Find on www.meetup.com

Outdoor Swimming Society
www.outdoorswimmingsociety.co.uk

Wild Swimming Website where you can find your nearest wild dip in natural waters. UK only.
www.wildswimming.co.uk

Wildway Bushcraft UK courses and information for cooking and living outdoors
www.wildwaybushcraft.co.uk

design and furniture

Alice in Scandiland Interior online shop based in Cornwall, UK, selling all things Scandi
www.aliceinscandiland.com

Brita Swedish design company creating plastic rugs for indoor and outdoor use, wool blankets, and bedding
britasweden.se

Finnish Design Shop Online store specializing in Nordic design
www.finnishdesignshop.com

Lotta Jansdotter Designer of beautiful Nordic patterns translated into home textiles, prints, and jewelry. From Åland originally but now based in New York. She's also written books on design and sewing.
www.jansdotter.com

Skandium Scandinavian design shop
www.skandium.com

Sigmar London Store and Nordic interior
design service
www.sigmarlondon.com

Svenskt Tenn Design store with
Josef Franks' patterns
www.svenskttenn.com

books

*The Open-Air Life: Discover the Nordic
Art of Friluftsliv and Embrace Nature
Every Day* by Linda Åkesson Mcgurk
(TarcherPerigee, 2022)

The Scandi Kitchen by Brontë Aurell
(Ryland Peters & Small, 2015)

North Wild Kitchen by Nevada Berg
(Prestel, 2018)

The Lagom Life: A Swedish Way of Living
by Elisabeth Carlsson (CICO Books, 2023)

Biophilia: You + Nature + Home by
Sally Coulthard (Kyle Books, 2020)

Waterlog by Roger Deakin (Vintage, 2011)—
a memoir about swimming throughout the
British Isles

Helena Halme's *Love on the Island* fiction
series set on Åland Islands

*Learning: The Owner's Manual for the
Brain* by Pierce Howard (William Morrow
Paperbacks, 2014)

*Lagom: The Swedish Art of Eating
Harmoniously* by Steffi Knowles-Dellner
(Quadrille Publishing Ltd, 2017)

*The Sustainable Home: Easy Ways to Live
with Nature in Mind* by Ida Magntorn
(Pavilion Books, 2022)

*Döstädning: The Gentle Art of Swedish
Death Cleaning* by Margareta Magnusson
(Canongate Books, 2020)

*Blue Mind: The Surprising Science That Shows
How Being Near, In, On, or Under Water Can
Make You Happier, Healthier, More Connected,
and Better at What You Do* by Wallace J.
Nichols (Back Bay Books, 2015)

Sisu: The Finnish Art of Courage by
Joanna Nylund (Gaia, 2018)

The Edible City: A Year of Wild Food
by John Rensten (Picador, 2016)

Blinded by Science by Matthew Silverstone
(Lloyd's World Publishing, 2011)

*Under the Open Skies: A Practical Guide to
Living Close to Nature* by Marcus Torgeby
(Simon & Schuster, 2020)

*Decluttering at the Speed of Life: Winning
Your Never-Ending Battle with Stuff* by
Dana K. White (Thomas Nelson, 2018)

documentaries

A Quiet Revolution, 2022, by The Gaia Foundation—about urban gardening

Call of the Forest: The Forgotten Wisdom of Trees, 2016

Hidden Life of Trees, 2020

Steam of Life (*Miesten Vuoro* in Finnish), 2010

read more

Kari Leibowitz—Stanford-trained heath psychologist, writer, and speaker
www.karileibowitz.com

The Nordic Mum—Online blog and podcast by Susanna Heiskanen
www.thenordicmum.com

Scandinavia Standard—one-stop info for all Scandiphiles
www.scandinaviastandard.com

The Swedish Society for Nature Conservation
naturskyddsforeningen.se

Visit Norway
www.visitnorway.com

Visit Finland
www.visitfinland.com

Swedish Tourist Association
www.swedishtouristassociation.com

Visit Iceland
www.visiticeland.com

Visit Denmark
www.visitdenmark.com

Faroe Islands Tourist Board
www.faroeislands.fo

index

Åkesson McGurk, Linda 64, 68

accessories 79
Advent 94–5, 96
adversity, dealing with 126–7
Alzheimers 25, 120
amaryllis 98
amino acids 15
Andersen, Hans Christian 8
antidepressants 130
antioxidants 16
apple juice, spiced 58, 61

Baker, Michelle 129
base layers 78
Bennett, Carrie 134
berries 17, 50
Bindefeld, Thommy 90, 92
bio-individuality 31
biophilia hypothesis 120
Blóðberg 53–4
Blue Mind science 29
the brain 12, 25, 28–9
bread 59
   grötbullar 44–5
   lomper 42–3
   pinbröd 59, 60
brown fat cells 30
bulbs 98, 105
burn out 129

cakes: kladdkaka 47
candles 94, 98, 109
   cinnamon-and orange-
      scented candles 102–3
cardiovascule disease 24,
   69, 120

celebrations, seasonal 38
chocolate: kladdkaka 47
Christmas 93, 96–101, 116
cities, foraging in 54–5
citrus ornaments 98–9
cleaning products 18
clothing 76–9
clutter 90, 91, 134
coffee 48, 59
cognitive function 12
cold-water swimming 30–1,
   72–5
collective mindset 130
consumerism 6, 135
cosmos 106
Coventry, Peter 31
crafting 98–9, 109
crowberries 54

death cleaning 90, 112–13
decluttering 8, 135
décor 89–91
decorations 7, 95, 99, 105,
   106, 109
Denmark 6, 15, 26, 64, 68
   burnout 129
   food and drink 42, 48, 94, 104
   Sankt Hans Aften 106
depression 123, 124
diabetes 15, 69
diet, Nordic 32–61
döstädning 90, 112–13
drinks: coffee 48
   glögg 39, 95
   spiced apple juice 58, 61

Easter 104, 105, 116
endorphins 24, 25, 30
Ericson, Estrid 90, 91
exercise 12–15, 134
Fair Isle pompom hat 110–11

fall 109
Faroe Islands 6, 40, 55, 64, 109
fika 44, 94–5, 116, 133
Finland 6, 15, 16, 64, 68, 133
   burn out 129
   coffee 48
   diet 47
   lakes 26
   saunas 22, 23, 25
   seasonal celebrations 96, 104,
      105, 106
   sisu 126–7
fires, making 80
fitness 12–15
flatbreads 42–3
Flaten, Lena 56, 58
flowers 98, 104, 106, 109
food 7, 32–61
foraging 8, 50–5, 56
forests 15, 16, 47, 50, 80
   forest bathing 67, 122
   tree hugging 122–3
Frank, Josef 90–1
Frankfurters 58
Fredagsmys 134
free radicals 16
friluftsliv 12, 15, 68–71, 82,
   116, 119
Frisk I Naturen 119–23
furniture 90, 91

garden therapy 120
glögg 39, 95
gloves 58
Grahn, Patrick 120
grötbullar 44–5
Gunnarsdóttir, Thorgerdur
   Anna 126
hat, Fair Isle pompom 110–11
Headicar, Anja 129
Health in Nature 119–23

heart disease 24, 69, 120
Heikkilä, Laura 16, 18–19
Heiskanen, Susanna 135
herbs 17
hibernation 134
the home 8, 84–113
Howard, Pierce J. 29
hugging trees 122–3
hugnaligt 109
hyacinths 98, 105
hygge 90, 91, 135

Ibsen, Henrik 68
ice bathing 30
Iceland 64, 96, 116, 126, 129, 130
    food and drink 40–1, 48, 53–4,
      55, 95
    swimming 27–8
Icelandic Forest Service 122
immune systems 64, 67
injuries 24
insulin resistance 15

Jante, Law of 130

kaffe paus 48
Karolinska Institute 69–70
kayaking 26–7
kjötsúpa 41
kladdkaka 47
knitting 109, 134
    Fair Isle pompom hat 110–11
Knuuttiila, Tiina 22–3, 127
kolbulle 59
kos 134
koseligt 64, 109
krabbelurer 58, 61
Lago-Wight, Erin 104–5
lagom 19, 31, 90, 91, 135
lamb soup 41
Law of Jante 130
Leibowitz, Kari 64, 82, 134

light 90, 95, 124–5, 133–4
lillajul 96
lomper 42–3
Løvoll, Synnevåg 70, 82–3
löyly 22, 24
lucia 96
Lutheranism 15
Luukkanen, Tanya 129

Magnusson, Margareta 112
make-up 20
materials, natural 90, 91
memory 12
mental health, nature and
    119–20
Midsummer 106, 116
mindfulness 34, 114–35
muscle mass, increasing 15
mushrooms 50, 53

nature 8, 15, 31, 62–83, 116
    bringing nature into your life
      82–3
    friluftsliv 12, 15, 56, 68–71, 82,
      116, 119
    Health in Nature 119–23
    nature therapy 120
    skincare and 16–17, 19
Nichols, Wallace J. 29
Nordic Council of Ministers 119
Norway 6, 15, 27, 92, 94, 96,
    106, 129
    food and drink 42–3, 48
    nature 27, 64, 67, 68, 69
Nystrom, Fredrik 30

oats 58
    grötbullar 44–5
ornaments 91, 98–9
osteoporosis 15
outdoors, time spent 15, 56–61,
    80, 134

overwhelm 97, 133
oxytocin 29, 123

pain relief 24
pancakes: *krabbelurer* 58, 61, 69
paperwhites 98
parasympathetic nervous
    system 7
perseverance 126
phototherapy 124
pikkujoulu 96
pinbröd 59, 60
pine decorations 99
plants 8, 16, 82, 86, 90, 91,
    109, 134
porridge 58
    grötbullar 44–5
potatoes: *lomper* 42–3
pullakahvi 133

relaxation 24, 133
resilience 8, 126–7, 135
rhubarb 55
Richardson, Dr. Miles 123
Rógvadóttir, Guðrun 109
rugs, cleaning in the snow 99

SAD (Seasonal Affective
    Disorder) 124
sauna culture 22–5
sausages 58
seasonal living 7, 8, 37–9,
    84–113, 134
self-care, definition of 7–8
shinrin-yoku 67, 122
shoes 79
Silverstone, Matthew 123
sisu 126–7, 135
Skarsgård, Alexander 130
skincare 16–21, 25
sleep 25

snow, cleaning rugs in 99
soup 58
  lamb soup 41
spiced apple juice 58, 61
spring 104–5
stinging-nettle tonic 20
storage 90
strength training 12, 15
stress 7, 24, 120, 133
summer 106
sun 133–4
sustainability 6, 91
Svenskt Tenn 90, 92
Sweden 6, 15, 23, 90, 105
  burnout 129
  food and drink 44–7, 48, 58
  nature 64, 67, 68, 120
  seasonal celebrations 96,
    104, 106
swimming 26, 27–8, 30–1, 72–5

table decorations 105
thermos 58
Thorgerdur Anna
  Gunnarsdóttir 126
Thorstenson, Linn 34
time out 133
tobacco plant 106
tongs 58
tonic, stinging-nettle 20
toxins, reducing 17
trees 105, 122–3
tulips 105

Unionen 120
utbränd 129

Vähäsarja, Kati 15
vihtu 24, 25
vitamin D 124–5
walks 133, 134

water 26–31, 72–5
waterproof layers 78–9
weather 8, 64
wellbeing 12–15
Whyte, Greg 72–4
wild swimming 72–5
window decorations 95
wine 54
  glögg 39, 95
winter 93–103, 134
work-life balance 116
World Happiness Report 6
wreath, simple wire 101

Þetta reddast 126

Credits

Glögg recipe on page 39 © **Maxine Clark**; *Lomper* recipe on page 42 © **Miisa Mink**; *Kladdkaka* recipe on page 47 © **Brontë Aurell**; Simple wire wreath project on pages 100–101 © **Christiane Bellstedt Myers**; Cinnamon and orange-scented candles in enamel mugs project on pages 102–103 © **Emma Hardy**; Fair Isle pompom hat proect on pages 110–111 © **Fiona Goble**

Picture credits

Adobestock.com:

struvictory: artworks and borders on pages 3, 4, 8, 11, 15, 16, 20, 24, 25, 28, 30, 31, 33, 34, 37, 38–45, 47, 48, 53–56, 58–59, 61, 63, 64, 67–69, 70, 76, 79, 80, 82, 85–86, 89, 90–92, 98–99, 101–106, 109–113, 115–116, 120, 122–127, 129, 130, 133, 134–139, 144; **Lars Johansson:** page 5; **Anton:** leaf artworks on pages 6, 12, 19, 50, 51, 105, 119; **Roxana:** page 9; **noka:** pages 22, 27, 29, 72, 74–75, 94, 95 below, 97 below; page 119 above; **nyul:** page 25; **Aleksei Potov:** pages 25–26; **terovesalainen:** page 28; **Juhku:** page 31; **Conny Sjostrom:** page 52; **Jarkko:** page 57; **Adrian:** page 62; **Florian Kunde:** page 65; **Andrei Baskevich:** page 66; **JFL Photography:** page 69; **pierrick:** page 73; **visualspectrum/Stocksy:** page 75; **tramper79:** page 77; **napa74:** page 78; **Sergii Mostovyi:** page 79; **Stephanie Frey:** page 80; **ppa5:** page 81; **Stephen W. Morris Photography/Stocksy:** page 93 below; **katarinagondova:** page 95 above; **geargodz:** page 106; **Arrlfx:** page 122; **Roman Babakin:** page 127 above; **sokko_natalia:** page 139; **Tamara Kulikova:** page 142

Debi Treloar: pages 2, 14, 15, 54, 70 above, 83, 92, 93 above, 98, 99 below, 108, 117, 118, 119, 121, 124, 134; **Daniel Farmer:** page 10; **Mark Scott:** pages 13, 86, 91, 113, 125, 128; **Stuart West:** pages 17, 18, 19; **Lucinda Symons:** page 20, **Jan Baldwin:** pages 21, 71; **Peter Cassidy:** pages 32, 35, 38, 42, 43, 45, 46, 60, 61 above, 107; **Richard Jung:** page 36; **Noel Murphy:** page 39; **Nassima Rothacker:** page 49; **Tara Fisher:** page 53; **David Merewether:** page 55; **Georgia Glynn-Smith:** pages 59, 61 below; **Catherine Gratwicke:** pages 84, 87, 88, 89, 105; **Caroline Arber:** pages 99 above, 100; **Debbie Patterson:** pages 102, 103; **Rachel Whiting:** page 104; **Joanna Henderson:** pages 109, 116, 131; **Terry Benson:** page 111 above; **Steve Painter:** page 114; **James Merrell:** page 132; **Martin Norris:** page 135; **Penny Wincer and Emma Mitchell:** page 135

acknowledgments

Oliver—for your calming words, good advice, and for patiently reading the many versions of my manuscripts.

My mom and my dad for showing me love through seasonal traditions and food, dragging me out for woodland foraging walks, and creating a stable and warm family environment full of *fika* moments.

My family in Sweden for inspiration, for advice, and for generally being a really great bunch.

CICO Books—Cindy, Jenny, Penny, Sally, Gordana—for giving me the chance to write another book and sharing my thoughts on self-care from a Nordic perspective, and Geoff Borin for his design.

For the many people who gave up their time to chat to me and share their valuable perspective on many things including specifically self-care and the Nordic way of life. In no particular order: Anja, Tiina, Michelle, Pia, Thorgerdur Anna, Gunnar, Marika, Richard, Gudrun, Peter, Miles, Lena, Sanna, Kari, Helga, Tanja, Thommy, Linn, Anna-Karin, Susanna, and Vanessa.

Ella—our Cavapoo who so patiently waited for her walks.